FAR OUT
AUSTRALIA

From Scratch in a Hatch
with Tales and Tips
to Rediscover the Land

Rod Kluzki

Far Out Australia

Copyright © 2016 Rado Folwarczny

Winnty Publishing

farout@winnty.com

ISBN-13: 978-0-9876214-0-5

ISBN-10: 0-9876214-0-8

Cover Art © Winnty

Rod Kluzki

Editor-in-chief: Belinda Holmes

Consultant Editor: Dorota Szczytnicka

All rights reserved. No part of this book may be reproduced in any form by any means without the express written permission of the author. While every effort is made to ensure the accuracy of information at the time of publication, changes in circumstances may occur. The publisher accepts no liability or responsibility to any person or organisation as a consequence of any reliance upon the information contained in this book. Characters portrayed in this book are based on real people but their names were changed.

To my wife, son and daughter,

and to all the great people on the road that never ends

In this book, you are:

- going on a 16,000-kilometre journey across Australia, but not before learning the hard way (Australia needs to be conquered on paper first)

- going through well- and less-known places, seeing that the paid attractions are not always the most worthy ones

- getting useful tips about how to get most with the least effort and money

- getting a rundown of outback and other interesting places

- hearing about crime stories, criminal plots and murder cases, such as those about missing tourists and underbelly celebs

- learning about history of boom and bust industries like pearling in Broome, diamonds on Lake Argyle, opals in Coober Pedy, gold in Stawell and Hill End and oil shale in Wollemi

- exploring difficult relations between European settlers and indigenous Aboriginal population and why modern Australia cherry-picks alternative ways to explain its history

- seeing the fun and pitfalls of seasonal work in the tropics of Western Australia

- reading about encounters with creatures such as spiders, crocodiles, and why you don't need to panic

- getting place tips for photographers

- exploring the whims of extreme whether such as monsoon rain, floods, snow, hail, and learning where they can take you by surprise

- learning how to explore the Red Centre icons like Uluru/Ayers Rock, Olgas/Kata Tjuta and Kings Canyon for as little money as possible

- climbing Australian mountains like Mount Bruce, Mount Nameless, Mount Sonder, St Mary's Peak, Mount Arapiles, Mount Stapylton, Mount Kosciuszko and learning interesting facts about them

- learning how a small conventional but well-prepared car can become priceless in overcoming harsh Australian conditions and make the travels efficient and fun

- seeing both the humorous and serious sides of low-budget travelling

- and generally getting a different perspective on a continent that is still full of mysteries.

The book is based on fifteen years of observations. The unpretentious, three-month journey serving as its backbone starts in Perth and goes through the Western Australian coast, Pilbara, Kimberley, Darwin, The Red Centre, South Australia, Victoria, and finishes on the threshold of Sydney.

Today everybody can rediscover Australia. It is one of the best-prepared countries for car touring but one that can often be unpredictable and treacherous, with many traps, not only aimed at your wallet. Some knowledge offered here will help overcome those challenges and—if you don't plan to do it yourselves—it will keep you informed and entertained.

From section two onward, the book contains illustrated maps, many Google map links, black and white images as well as the route with kilometres, fuel estimates and the travel budget.

Contents

Preface — 13

I. Turning Upside Down — 15

1 Cook's Syndrome: Australia Is More — 17
2 Underdogs to Explorers — 17
3 Everybody Can: No Pain No gain — 21
4 Crash Course in Australian Basic Education — 24
5 Driving Thingybob and the Holy Licence — 26
6 Indigenous versus Mainstream: Take I — 29
7 The Case *Nullius* and *Terra* Mabo — 31
8 Hatch, Hatch, Hatchback — 34
9 Slowly, Slowly Catchee Possum — 37
10 Pavlova — 41
11 Useful Tips and Off We Go — 42

II. Perth to Broome — 47

12 At the Bottom of the Sea: Pinnacles — 47
13 Spider from Nerren Nerren — 50
14 Pouring Buckets: Monsoon Rain — 53
15 Sea to Mountains — 55
16 Iron Prince of Pilbara: Tom Price — 59
17 The Nanny — 62
18 Walking On Ore: Karijini National Park — 64

19 Salt, Tibet And the Prophecy of Port Hedland	69
20 Great Sandy Desert	72
21 Indigenous versus Mainstream: Take II	75
22 Tourist Broome	78

III. Broome to Darwin   83

23 "That Funny Hotel": From Fitzroy to Halls	83
24 Vanishing Tourists Business	88
25 United We Fall	90
26 Of Crocodiles and Men: Take I	93
27 Castration as a Job: Kununurra	96
28 Sea in the Desert: Lake Argyle	101
29 Customs and Public Holidays: NT Border	107
30 Spa Time: Katherine is Hot, Douglas is Cool	109
31 Darwin in a Nutshell	115

IV. Darwin to Alice Springs   117

32 Where You Only Swim in a Pool: Kakadu	117
33 Of Crocodiles and Men: Take II	121
34 Flying in the Bush: Mataranka	122
35 Alice in Wander Land	126
36 Road to Nowhere: West MacDonnell Ranges	130
37 On a Bike Through Desert	135

V. Alternative Look At Red Centre   139

38	Where Things Howl: Uluṟu aka Ayers Rock	139
39	Sexy Walls: Kata Tjuṯa and Kings Canyon	146
40	Coroner on Vacation	147
41	Busting Dingo	148
42	Where Mad Max Drove: Breakaways	150

VI. White Bloke Down a Pit   153

43	Opal Land: the Ingenuity of Coober Pedy	153
44	Indigenous Versus Mainstream: Take III	158
45	Welcome and Piss Off: On How to Find ...	160
46	Firecracker Town: Woomera	166

VII. Port Augusta to Melbourne   169

47	Tough Luck Mountains: Ikara-Flinders Ranges	169
48	Adelaide in a Nutshell	174
49	Fifty Thousand Years Ago: Naracoorte	175
50	All Seasons in One Day: Grampians	177
51	What Guides Won't Say: Real Peaks of Grampians	180
52	Clay and Whales: Great Ocean Road	185
53	Melbourne in a Nutshell	187
54	Uncle Chopper And Papa Rog	187

VIII. Melbourne to Sydney   193

55	Mister Ricketts' Beautiful Soul	193
56	North Over the Hill Country	195

57 Why Mount Kosciuszko	196
58 Canberra in a Nutshell	202
59 Mountains Upside Down	202

IX. Golden Epilogue — 207

60 Where Freedom Begins: Hill End	207
61 It's Panning Out	210
62 In Which Otto Won his Lotto	212
63 Big Smoke	215

APPENDIX — 219

Glossary	221
Map	225
Noteworthy Mountains and Peaks	227
Route and Refuelling	229
Travel Budget Hints	235
Not to forget	237
Bibliography	239

INDEX — 241

It's cool and hot, wherever you're not

far-out
Adj. Slang
1. Great or cool; extraordinary;
2. An expression of amazement, approval or delight;
2. Very hard to understand, strange, arcane;
3. Extremely unconventional;
4. Unusual or eccentric; very advanced;
6. When postpositive bizarre or avant-garde;
7. Intoxicated;
8. Excellent; wonderful;
9. Offbeat; radical or extreme.

Various dictionaries

rediscovering
Gradually starting to understand something that was once thought to have been *discovered*, but later classified to have *not been discovered*, so that in the end it wouldn't really matter, because it has always been there.

Author

Preface

Shortly before the beginning of the third millennium, a runaway horse had set out on a quest to swim from the South Australian coast down to Antarctica. A rescue crew made of a large number of volunteers could not figure out how to pull the hapless animal out of water for many hours, and before they did, it had almost drowned. From that moment, I longed to take a glimpse of a country where horses are lined up on seashores, ready to charge for the breaking swells without warning, so that ever greater formations of rescuers followed in their tracks to save them. It is almost impossible to judge the world by the daily news. So I went there, with one backpack, naive expectations, almost no money of my own and a rather normal portion of common sense. My then-girlfriend-now-wife later joined me for a journey that still lasts. Despite Australia's reputation as an expensive country, it can still be toured on a very reasonable budget, in quite a normal car, with cheap, average equipment. What I didn't have, but could have used, was a bottom-up information starter-pack that would tell me more or less everything to quench the initial thirst for information, to help make better decisions in preparation for the trip and present the fun stuff about the country and its incredibly intriguing history and geography. Every place has a soul and every stone has a story to tell. Travelling is an ultimate eye-opener. I am deliberately putting aside the politically correct, carefully presented, neatly combed Australia as it is sold around the world, because a lot of it is tourism marketing, and I am stubbornly focusing on the less-known, unofficial version of it, the one you only start to unveil after a few years of living there, when you manage to free yourselves of big cities with poisonous souls, and go inland, meeting locals who will tell you more than all the travel guides combined, the sort of stuff you won't find in any official news portal. Australia is extraordinary and mysterious and that's what makes it so worthwhile.

Bon voyage!

I. Turning Upside Down

I am landing in Sydney and Australia is lying at my feet.

The TV crews are getting their gear ready, the thudding brass band and sexy cheerleaders are in full swing, my name is in the headlines and the red carpet is ready to roll. The colourful shimmering glitters have filled the sky and made it into a splendid spectacle of joyful celebration.

Hardly off the plane, I am swallowed by a crowd of greedy journalists. Their microphones and cameras are kissing me all over my head. The whole country has been brought to a standstill.

I am the ONE they have all been waiting for.

Then the music stops.

In a cheap backpackers' at the very fringe of a big city, I wake up with streaks of sweat running down my foreheads. It's my first night in Australia.

But let's not jump the gun. I'm getting ahead of myself. First things first.

1
Cook's Syndrome: Australia Is More

At the corner of Park and College Streets, in more or less the middle of a green city patch called Hyde Park, in the continent's largest city, there is a grand statue of a prominent man. He wears a grey, unbuttoned coat that appears to be stained because it has been there—sun and rain—for a long time.

To the eye of the casual observer, the relatively modest five-metre or so stone figure doesn't seem to be anything out of ordinary. A large plaque at the base reveals it "marks the site of another plaque" that presumably has been stolen. The captain got this one instead. Cook was kind of first—a "Bradbury" of the eighteenth century who raised his hand and coined the face to an unknown continent.

He was not the first, he was not the last. To better understand it, Australia has to be discovered time and time again. And ideally, there need to be crowds of discoverers.

Because here they are, the omnipresent images pinned to our subconscious repository of the Antipodean preconceptions: a kangaroo, a koala, intense goldish sunset on a blue horizon, face-painted Aboriginal people with boomerangs hopping around a fire for tourists, the Opera House, the Harbour Bridge, grinning students in marketing catalogues. Then money in excess, lunch breaks spent surfing at Manly, Bondi and Santa—Santa-bloody-Clause in swimmers in the very middle of "winter".

Stereotypes? We're touching down. This time with no ovations.

2
Underdogs to Explorers

Before I went there, I had only met two Australians in the flesh in my whole life. It's as if they had been in short supply, or the world had run out of them. Then, when I first arrive in Sydney, a whistling turbaned taxi driver with an accent totally unknown to me takes me from the airport to my first hostel. After finding out where I come from, he pauses his tune and utters, "Lendl. Nedved," then purses his lips again and carries on. The air is different—warm and wet, as if drawn from the sea—and there are strange noisy birds with even weirder squealing sounds everywhere. White parrots and brown ferals called miner birds.

I get used to Sydney more or less instantly; after a month I don't mind bus stop benches facing off streets to make it harder for me to see the arriving buses, cyclists notoriously ignoring red lights and water in taps so hot I can brew a coffee in it. The city icons, blah; its cultural life, blah, blah; the First State Metropolis. A big yawn. It's advertised everywhere.

Suddenly I am a part of that pulse, the grandeur. I am so cool, I am so in. I own everything around, yet nothing belongs to me. The skyscrapers' night silhouettes, pulsating shopping centres, the variety. As if all the world has somehow made it to this one place for me. Nevertheless, I couldn't wait for the triumphant moment when I challenge all that, and rewrite history with my own trip. But not just yet.

Cook must have been an incredible persona to reach a land so far away from his home on just a pile of nailed wooden planks with some sails affixed to them, having but a sextant as his main navigation tool. He kind of popped in by chance at that, after observing the transit of Venus— his main job. He was to check the unknown southern piece of land already spotted years ago by the Dutch and the French. So he did. Once he was here, though, all he had to do was to get off his ship. He arrives as quite an extraordinary overseas explorer.

When I want to properly set foot on the continent, my status is figuratively tottering on a small dinghy still somewhere between Kuala Lumpur and Jakarta. Moreover, it sails right into a major storm. I can already sense the rising swell of the ocean. After about three months, I am coming to the conclusion that I don't own the continent at all; it is the continent that owns every inch of me. I arrive as quite an ordinary overseas student.

Student visas and relating fees, exorbitant education costs, selective commercial insurance, unfunny agents living off my commission, astronomical rents, sleepless nights. The fourth month, my mind is already in a loop, thinking how to bust myself out of that vicious cycle and remain in sane spirit.

I go to the immigration office for advice. "G'day. Howsitgoin? Can you please give me some kind of a—writ—so that I can, just in the philosophical sense, roam free?"

I get a decent answer immediately. *Get lost*.

Or, *get used?* Something like that, because when seeing my distraught face, they call me *mate* and have my arms loaded with a huge stash of beautifully tinted forms so that in my free time from dusk to sunrise, I can read them, study them, fill them in and out, sign them, check them, provide more details, then read and study them again, fill in and sign them, recheck and send them one after another to authorised bureaucratic institutions.

After two centuries of British influence, Australia came out rather bureaucratic—but in saying that—in a very romantic and innocent way. While in many parts of Europe, the office rats would have long scratched your eyeballs out of their lateral rectus muscles for not filling out a form correctly, here the patient officers collect every detail, right down to the size, colour, and smell of your right sock, and you can even ask questions. They don't even have to think much. The system does it for them. For example:

"Hi, I lost my wallet and need new driver's licence."

"It's twenty-five dollars."

"Yes. But I lost my wallet with everything in it."

"That's fine. You can pay by card."

"Yes. But I lost my wallet, and my cards were also in it."

"Okay, you can pay by cash then. There is an ATM around the corner—"

"Yes, but—". Anyway.

And in between that filling in and sending out, we—because there are two of us—get acquainted with the local mentality, take some liking to the Australian accent, form opinions about the local system of government, education, culture, work ethic, food, transport; what's driving the streets, what is all the rage on TV, and later on even memorise the name of the prime minister.

The last mentioned—or rather, one of his underlings—finally informs us, in a very special memorandum, that the government approved our expedition plans and from now on we can regard ourselves promoted in status—from alien subjects from another planet to a semi-domesticated breed of vassals who can freely roam but should not jump too high. They call it PR, which everywhere else stands for Public Relations, but here it means Permanent Residency. Yes, getting PRed is equivalent to taking off a huge iron ball off the right foot—or left, depending on which one you rely on more.

In a short addendum inscribed at the bottom of the page, in rather tiny caps starting "Conditions Apply", the PM also informs us that while a new discovery expedition is welcome, he's certainly NOT contributing a single bloody cent, let alone a dollar.

Fair enough.

And that leads us to the second concern. A financial one. If one is not a millionaire's brat, or doesn't have the Crown behind the back, some kind of work will almost certainly be welcome.

We have nothing to lose and so we pack up and get a no-frills ticket to the opposite coast, as far as we can while we still have some cash. There, in Perth, WA, we'll try to resurrect ourselves and then travel across Australia back to Sydney.

It's a five-hour flight, enough time to admire the endless beautiful plains, so flat that surely it's going to be a breeze to cross them. With a brand new toothbrush in the backpack, a few books, and a meagre debit card, we can't wait for the journey to start.

As a matter of fact, it has already started.

3
Everybody Can: No Pain No gain

"Do you have experience cleaning bogs, mate?"

"I beg your pardon?"

"What experience do you have cleaning toilets?" asks the bulky-looking Lebanese supervisor, who does a sort of recruitment while finishing his morning tea consisting of a fresh doughnut.

"Well, I—I did it—I did it once—at home—" I reply, somewhat surprised.

Wrong answer. High-level employment questions like that should be met with a wide smile, beaming enthusiasm and an assertion that cleaning *dunnies* has always been the most fulfilling part of my entire career, and it is something I definitely want to stay with until I retire. I'm just lovin' it.

"Yeah, you need the local experience."

Hell, aren't bogs the same everywhere? It's true that in North America and Taiwan, I sat on bowls full of big lake of water, and if the Tsar Bomba hit the surface from the wrong angle the resulting splash didn't mushroom from the toilet only because my bum acted as a cork stopper. Australia adopted the European system, like a small fishpond, the surface of which can additionally be camouflaged with a bit of toilet paper for gentler impact when your short-range ballistic missiles reach the target. In that regard I felt very much at home and couldn't see a problem.

If you abandon the official line and say something stupid like, "Um, I just need some dough to travel, mate," it won't work. It goes without saying for better jobs in particular.

It would be silly to think that with the "domesticated alien" status we're going to rank as high as we used to back at home. Quite the contrary. It might be a serious ride down the career path, especially in the beginning. But who cares? Embrace it because short-term shitty jobs are excellent opportunities to experience the continent from its very bottom, as it were, and shouldn't that be on every true explorer's list? It provides a whole wealth of opportunities and invaluable insights.

Why would I want a high-flying job when I am going to quit after only a few weeks? It's like skipping the whole foreplay before making love out of habit, or arriving at a fancy restaurant, snubbing the entrée, the soup, the main dish and leaping right onto the sweet dessert, devouring it greedily and demonstratively burping in front of the entire floor.

Surely something will be missing. Skipping this crucial stage prevents you from getting the whole picture.

Kitchen hand will be a fantastic start!

The restaurant is run by an Indian guy called Paul. Paul, who can reliably distinguish between Danish and Norwegian because he used to work in Sweden, never has any supplies on stock until the very moment he takes an order. Once he knows what he needs, he hysterically starts to boss around his kitchen hand—me—who starts desperate rallies to the nearby shopping centres. "Quick! Quick! Go! Go! Before the table leaves!" Be it chicken breasts, cauliflower lettuce, veal, a plastic strainer or spatula because he has just broken one when killing a cockroach.

While that is being looked after, he proceeds to supervise his kitchen staff, occasionally unloading a parsley sprig from a used plate returned to the kitchen, and beautifully arranges it on top of a new plate that his American waitress is delivering to a customer.

"Savings matter, mate."

"How about the steaks? Did you get them too?" he asks me on

3 Everybody Can: No Pain No gain

my return. "Didn't Luke tell you we needed them?"

Luke, a plump naturalised English cook with an unshaven stubbled face, arrives at work about two hours late that morning because he got entangled in a pub brawl last night—quite innocently, he says. Standing between two local skips who dared question his pom heritage, he thought this was an excellent opportunity to teach them a lesson or two about manners:

"Strewth, mate! Your bathroom home-brew's the best in the world, eh?" he mocked them in a poor imitation of their own accent.

All he remembers next are heavy boot soles walking all over his face. Two fresh brass-knuckle-carved grooves are stamped on his swollen cheeks, while a third adorns his nose along its full length. He can only see us through one of his eyes.

"Calling me a cunt and stomping my face didn't help them one fucking bit, mate," he still maintains through the bruised corner of his red mouth, going about his usual business.

Luke works in hospitality, which means if he's not dead, he has to show up. That, however, doesn't stop everybody wondering how on earth he is still able to stand. With Luke, the only plausible explanation is the legendary British stamina that has made it possible to inhabit a continent as inhospitable as Australia, and if not for him "none of you bloody losers would be around today". And he always has a good piece of fatherly advice. "Go home, get some Steven Seagal movies, and beat the shit out of your hamster."

*

The west coast of Australia is different in one particular way. Unlike the eastern states, the sun actually doesn't rise from the sea but from the land mass horizon, and beautifully illuminates the whole city of Perth in the morning.

A lady in a recruitment agency is going out of her way to assure me that every two minutes a new plane lands in WA, full of overzealous immigrants with only one objective—to take working opportunities away from me the moment they touch down. I shouldn't risk not accepting her offer. "You'll be a part of a cleaning squad and you cover all your working expenses. You'll get hourly rates and you need an ABN," the business number as a prerequisite. You'll be a cleaning businessman.

The cleaning of the conference rooms starts at four am, finishes at nine. By seven I am done and go home. I lie down in my makeshift bed and wake up at about noon. I open my eyes and my mind slowly starts to kick in. A hangover? I am not sure, but a few more bucks are landing in my bank account towards the end of the week.

If a better, more sophisticated job is at stake, one needs to pay particular attention to the CV, better known here as a résumé, although most often without accents. It is a bit like breast augmentation: it needs to look good on the surface but what is in it is less important. A good first impression is what counts, plus references from those who knew me from the past, boundless self-confidence and a strong desire to crown life by pounding keyboards of a large corporation until death does us part. Then, after three months, I find it is totally and completely incongruent with my life philosophy of a nomad and I simply quit.

What follows is probably the most intense and spiritually rewarding educational phase of my life. A true crash course.

4
Crash Course in Australian Basic Education

The learning curve in a strange land is much steeper. It's a little bit like being born again and looking at the new world through the eyes of an innocent infant. The world seems to be familiar and is alleviated by instincts, but up until now I've been in my mother's womb without any real experience of life outside. I've been uncompromisingly pushed out, landing on big cold metal weighing scales. If I get a job, it will be a boob to suck on to grow and get bigger, with only one slight difference: instead of getting on my feet in two years, I will need to do it in two months. And in another six months, I'll have to go through a development cycle that normally takes ten years. Observation is my strongest weapon.

Cleaning a local public school, I learn "on the go". I read notice boards about reconciliation efforts between the indigenous and mainstream population—a topic that, together with racial tolerance, has been around for a few generations now, in the sense that the colonisers disposed of the cultural identity of the indigenous people.

The next room is science. There is a large paper box with some light inside, where new life is hatching from under the white fragile eggshells. At first they are round and full, but every day they crack more and more as their habitants try to reach daylight. The chooks will greet the world soon.

I become two years older in the next room. I learn about the solar system—Jupiter's diameter is eleven times larger than that of Earth—and read about lives of famous astronomers—Tycho Brahe is listed higher than Copernicus.

I observe a full range of fruits and veggies all across the floor, giving me a perfect idea of what had been on the menu today. Combined with some sand, lumps of dirt brought from the playground—it's not practical to take shoes off—and remnants of what once used to be writing tools and paper sheets, the picture of the school day is nearly complete.

My quiet contemplation is interrupted by a teacher. She has come back for some stuff she forgot when tidying up her desk, because from tomorrow she will be on her long service leave—a long paid holiday break after fifteen years of service. She is stopping in Bali and then going to Europe, which in the popular parley of many means somewhere *starting in England and ending in Germany, with France halfway in-between.*

"How about going around Australia?" I am curious.

"Far out! I wish I could do that. But I don't have time!" Australians tend to go overseas. "You probably know more about Australia than I do," she giggles.

To which I reply that I find locals very knowledgeable about both. Older generations mainly. An Australian friend of mine went for a tour of Iran without knowing anybody there. He just wanted to see the country. Despite common fears of hostility toward westerners, what he came across were the most hospitable and friendly people he has ever met, a beautiful ancient country with quite good, cheap inland airline connections. And he only spoke English at that.

"What a disappointment for the official mainstream doctrine," he said. "Right now our prime minister is in America, doing a certain amount of sucking up to the Yanks". But this was the only thing he hated about his government. We met him in Slovakia, hiking in the mountains of High Tatras. when he noticed gypsies chopping firewood in a national park. "Oh, they are like Aborigines."

5
Driving Thingybob and the Holy Licence

There is just one more thing to sort out before getting out the door: a valid local driver's licence, which is also an ID. If you happen to come from "the right" country, they will just swap it for an Aussie one. Otherwise, too bad. Once you are a permanent resident—a "domesticated alien"—you should stop using the overseas licence after a short period. Then you might need to go through another crash course.

Theory comes first. There is some practical stuff like drinking prevention: how many beers you can park and still hit the road? Two for Wayne, one for Sheila. Or questions like: when the road surface is wet, the braking distance required is a) shorter b) same c) longer? Longer. Or: why do you need to stop before a railway track? Because trains are heavy and take a long time to stop.

Australian traffic lights are on a 24/7 regime, which means all

5 Driving Thingybob and the Holy Licence

around the clock, seven days a week and fifty-two weeks a year. If by any miracle they ever stop flashing, this kind of situation is so unusual, nobody seems to recall priority to the right. For a few minutes, it becomes Thailand. All cars, no matter where they are, stop so drivers can scratch their heads. As long as the stream of cars on the main road is winning, all who are in it happily chug along until one of the cars on the adjacent road is bold enough to push through. Then the cars behind it follow suit until one of the braver drivers on the other road finds a gap and forces the cycle back where it started. And so it goes on until police arrive. They don't exactly have to run the intersection because by now the company in charge of the traffic lights has fixed the light computer. The traffic lights are back in action.

Back to the driver's licence. One can get an international version of an overseas driving licence that can be used for some time in Australia, but they look rather dodgy. The police officer presented with such a document—usually a folded worn-down A5 brochure in French—during a routine road check, will raise his eyebrows and mumble something to the effect of, "What the hell—?"

If I need to go for a driving test in New South Wales, I need to show up in a car. Now, how can I arrive in my own car, if in theory I don't have a local driving licence? A bit of a catch-22 to foreigners but never mind. There are plenty of car rentals. One-day rates are relatively expensive and so it's better to rent it for a few days and combine it with a nice trip afterwards.

Once I have booked the exam and rented the car, I arrive to the organisation in charge of traffic management. It's a different organisation in each state and it keeps changing. After filling in some forms and showing some papers like insurance for the car I've just hired, my driver's licence translation, card details, I am escorted to the vehicle by an officer wearing a shiny yellow-orange vest. He casually asks how I am—good—but he doesn't really look he cares at all. For the next quarter of an hour or so he is going to assess my driving skills. He is going to meticulously tick all the boxes on his checklist. And I don't blame him. He has been here since the morning, my driving test is about his sixth, for the fourth day in a row he has been annoyed by rookies who know bugger-all about changing gears, overtaking, backing up, parking, who stomp the gas pedal too abruptly, brake too violently, don't look in the rear-view mirror, passionately cuddle the steering wheel and what's worse: enter the wrong side of the road. Of course, that's not me. I've already driven thousands of kilometres in Australia and New Zealand, right? Some mistakes are regarded minor, only reducing my score, while others will be punished by almost a certain fail. The officer needs to tick them all. While performing a three-point-turn in a narrow lane somewhere on the city fringe, I'm halfway through the test.

The officer only gives me his judgement from the safety of his chair behind the counter, shielded by a thick glass window. He is prints a certificate. "Mate, you didn't pass," he says calmly. Apparently I went both too fast and too slow and I didn't let go a car from the opposite direction when turning right, even though it was in another lane. He takes out a pair of large pliers and punches a half-inch hole in my existing licence, issuing a new one in an act of consolation: the Learner licence for an additional fee.

"From now on you can only drive with somebody who has a full licence," sounds his advice.

"How am I going to get the car back to the rental company?" I ask.

"Well, you need somebody with a full licence."

"I don't know anybody—with a full licence. In fact, I don't know *anybody* here."

In two weeks, the same rental company readily lends me the same car using the same old licence, although now visibly and officially "holey". An average Australian rental assistant doesn't give a damn about holes in overseas driver's licences.

The testing station counter has a queue. An argument is going on between the officer in a yellow-orange vest and a young aspiring driver from Asia. The latter has just been told he had failed.

The same officer with an equally bored expression greets me from behind the counter. It's down to formalities: driver's licence, car details, insurance, etc.

"Who drove you in, mate?" he asks casually, while his eyes don't move from the forms.

"A friend?"

"Sure."

We leave the garage and take a different route. The officer's strained look does not bode well.

At the safety of the counter again, he informs me I failed. This time, he says, I almost ran over a pedestrian.

"Who's taking you home?"

"A friend."

6
Indigenous versus Mainstream: Take I

When it comes to history, there is this one peculiar oddity: Australians don't seem to know with a hundred per cent certainty whether their ancestors discovered their own country or not. The stories are full of this pioneer and that pioneer first having come upon this spot and that place, saw that promontory first and explored that cove and mapped something else: noble grand discoveries. We came, we saw, we claimed.

Then—in 1988—there was a big celebration to commemorate bicentenary after the arrival of the Phillip's First Fleet and they needed to re-enact that event in a pompous show, also using Aboriginal performers, and this was to be for the eyes of the entire world. And one can imagine the poor choreographer handing out the parts.

"Now you people here are going ashore with oxen and sheep, the next group—men with heavy boxes, hens, grain, corn, the guards follow with convicts over there—" then he turns to a bunch of native actors recruited for the purpose, "—and you guys are going to welcome us from the shore with your spears and then you're going to—"

"That wasn't a welcoming gesture—" retorts somebody from that crowd suddenly.

"—pardon?"

"That wasn't a 'hi'. We wanted you to disappear, TO GET THE HELL OUT OF HERE!"

"Well—that's a—bit of a—diversion from the line—" he stutters, puzzled, putting his specks on to consult the script.

Then somebody even bolder at the back of the group shouts:

"It was an invasion! We've been here for fifty thousand years!"

And so, it was only in the 1980s that this voice was finally heard and cast some doubts on the discovery claim. And hey, can't you and I discover Australia now too?

But then, if not discovery, what was is? Yes, there was violence, guns, the lot. But technically it doesn't live up to the whole picture. An army is usually invading something, but there was none. They even brought their own slaves. A "friendly invasion" then, or a "late discovery" maybe? An "undiscovery"? Argh! I am totally confused. What was it? I want to know! One thing is sure. Anything you say on this topic, one of the sides will say to you you're full of it.

A lawyer friend of mine wanted to save me from my frustration once and, over a beer, offered an explanation in the form of two seemingly unrelated stories. The first one starts in 1770 when Cook first sets foot on the local soil and the second one—about two hundred years later—when a person named Eddie Koiki Mabo feels the royal moccasin on his shoulder blade. Here are very laid-back, heavily lightened up, slightly convoluted pub versions of both mixed up in one.

7
The Case *Nullius* and *Terra* Mabo

When the famous English globetrotter James Cook descended from his boat in New Holland in 1770, it was one of his many amazing discoveries. Apart from noticing numerous queer animals, which were hastily painted on parchment by his associates, he couldn't help noticing some very strange men as well. They were unclad and they didn't respond to his interpreter, whose language skills up to this point had got them nicely along the whole Pacific:

"Aloha!"

No response.

"Aloha! Aloha!"

Nothing.

The natives threw a few baffled looks, stood up, and taking their wooden spears, slowly walked away. After the next few futile attempts at communication, Cook continued to observe them, finally concluding that savages lived within very modest means, they had neither shelters nor fences and that he was in *terra nullius*—no man's land, an empty uncivilised country not owned by anyone.

The absence of fences in particular was taken as a noteworthy observation. Later that evening, the Union Jack was erected and Cook, pressing his foot against the seashore rock, observed a romantic sunset. With his elbow resting on his knee, and looking through his binoculars into the far sea beyond, in solemn contemplation he opened his lips and just for himself whispered a never recorded question, "If it's not theirs, whose is it?"

*

I. Turning Upside Down

Nearly two hundred years later, an indigenous activist—except he didn't know he was one yet—was making his way home from work. Eddie Koiki Mabo was an ordinary man living in Murray Island in Queensland's Torres Strait. He had happily inhabited his small shack for many years and enjoyed a quiet and humble life with all the simple pleasures the Crown had to offer to its loyal subjects in the subdued domains. Today is today and tomorrow is tomorrow. A little smile can save the day no matter what, and he didn't give a damn about politics, trusting only what he could see and feel right in front of his eyes.

One day, a rainforest pigeon delivered him a letter with a beautiful official stamp portraying a middle-aged lady called Elizabeth. The last sentence of it plainly informed him that within two years, a brand new multi-lane fancy road was going to be whizzing through the middle of his humpy's living room.

"None of that! Over my fucking dead body!" he shouted, and in the sudden thrust of emotion he proceeded tearing the document to pieces, at the same time fiercely waving off annoying swarms of flies from his sweaty neck.

"Fucking government!" he snorted. "You're not getting away with that! I am doing something about it! NOW!" And he did. He went to a local pub and got plastered.

And as he was leaning against the bar, giving the bored bartender his story, it caught the ear of a stranger, a gentleman sitting at the nearby table.

"Pardon me, gentlemen," he said, "perhaps I can help. I know a bit about America and how they've already dealt with the problem there." And he went on to a lengthy description of the ordeals the Native Americans had to go through.

"—and with this, they had to prove they had their own law and the paleface had trespassed that law. The court eventually accepted the notion and their claim to the stolen land became legitimate. You have to go down the same path." Despite a headache in the morning, Eddie sought the mysterious scholar again.

7 The Case Nullius and Terra Mabo

"You need to prove you had some kind of rules to govern yourselves, some kind of a code that the British have violated. You might have scribbled it down somewhere, leather, rocks, stones, trees?"

"I don't know," he replied politely.

"Something you used to rule your lives, maintain peace and order; some—you know—some customary law you had passed on from generation to generation and wrote down somewhere, anything! Anything?"

"We only painted," he said, and added to make his point clearer: "We never wrote." The professor took off his glasses and rubbed his temples.

"Well, then we have a problem."

He visited Mabo again in a month's time.

"Even if you didn't write anything, somebody else might have. Wasn't there anybody else who wrote something down for you?"

Eddie thought. He remembered his grandfather saying once that his parents had met some very strange people. They liked to share everything and they read from a big book and asked questions that nobody could answer. "They laughed at us, saying an octopus couldn't be God. But he is. My father taught me."

"The missionaries! That's it!" exclaimed the prof in joy. "They wrote. They wrote a lot! We really have to find those manuscripts."

Neither of them had the faintest idea then they had just started a ten-year journey through the labyrinth of lawsuits.

*

The main and most crucial point of the whole dispute was to prove that the aboriginal people owned their lands in the true sense, which is described as Native Title to Land. It wasn't easy, but in the end it was upheld by court in a breakthrough decision.

Mabo, however, didn't live to see the final verdict. Without ever knowing it, he managed to win the most significant precedent in the legal history of Australia. It was named after him: the Mabo case.

From around 1992, the natives were able to lay claims to regain their stolen lands. The disputes were rather complex. The government has withheld the right to lands that were acquired "legally" in compliance with the anti-discrimination laws of the 70s. The trials took six years in average and many claimants didn't live to see the end. What was left in most cases was mainly desert and wasteland of little value. The lucrative lands like green pastures, parts of towns or areas with mineral deposits in the possession of big businesses were already untouchable. In a gesture that costs nothing the natives are often called "traditional custodians" in spite of the fact that they have no rights to those lands and not a remote chance of ever getting them back.

Nevertheless, Mabo changed Australia like no other before him. The conservative part of Australia tried to overturn the precedent, but it could no longer be undone.

Three years after Mabo's death, an unknown perpetrator desecrated his tomb. Mabo was buried again in his native Murray Island, this time like a king.

8
Hatch, Hatch, Hatchback

The Australian travel equation is simple—one and one are two, but no matter what, we need to be prepared and have three things ready: water—always and everywhere; head cover and sun protection, also always and everywhere, because sunstroke isn't our friend; and finally, spare tyre and toolbox, whether or not we plan to go far beyond the main roads. We can't prepare for the unpredictable, of course, but we can at least minimise possible trouble. Should we want to go north, "winter" months will be more suitable for it. They start in June. Winter and summer in Australia is more tropical than those from the northern hemisphere may expect. The seasons are better known as dry season in winter and wet season in summer, especially in the northern parts of Australia where the concept of winter is completely different, and what they think is cold, northern hemisphere residents would call positively balmy. The weather patterns can, however, be thrown out of sync sometimes, especially with the El Niño pattern. We might get stuck because of floods or fires. Then the roads are closed or blocked without mercy. Nature just doesn't give a flying duck about your travel plans.

As for the infrastructure, only larger city centres were laid out before the great invention of the car. So if you work there, public transport will more than do, unless you are keen on spending half of your pay on parking fees and fines. To be mobile and flexible somewhere out there outside the big conglomerates, however, a car is an absolute must. From the 1950s, towns were shaped for them and many people love their cars to such an extent they use them like outdoor shoes, leaving them in the shopping mall car parks, then walking barefooted or in thongs, not the G-strings, mind you, but a pair of light slippers. By the way, seeing somebody's bare feet in a shopping centre is regarded more natural than pair of socks in sandals, which is like putting a red-lettered sign over my neck saying:

I AM A WEIRDO FROM OVERSEAS.

So what's there to choose from? There is plenty.

"You're going to travel, mate?" asks a young pumped-up sales rep at a second-hand car dealership.

"Well, first I'd like to—"

"—you need a Ford Falcon or Holden Commodore, mate," he says in a say-no-more tone. He stretches his hand and says, "It has to be big so you can sleep in it, you know what I mean?"

I look around.

I. Turning Upside Down

"This is what you need, and it's a bargain," a real bargain, I am told.

"Can I take it for a test drive? I know a car mechanic nearby, I'd be back in an hour. If it's okay, I'll buy."

Two previous ones said no. This one says yes and will hold my driver's licence as deposit so he knows I am coming back. If I am pulled up by police, I simply tell them he has got my licence and everything will be sweet. "That's normal," he says.

The car mechanic shakes his head. "No bloody way, mate. The gearbox is leaking, that's the downside of this model. If it comes apart while you're on the road, nobody is going to piece it together. The aircon doesn't work anyway. Look, buy something reliable, even small, without an aircon. When I was young, there were no bloody aircons and we lived. Toyota. You might pay a few extra bucks but it retains value once you want to get rid of it."

We return the Falcon. "Very good car. But no thank you." We can't buy it yet anyway. In fact, we're still waiting for money from the rental bond in Sydney. We are hunting Toyotas for the next two days. The more time it takes, the more stress descends on us. We'll get a trouble to get to work without a car and if we don't have a job we won't have enough money to buy a car soon. One mistake and we're broke.

We've spent the last week staying with an Australian friend we met in Europe.

"Be careful. All car dealers are criminals. Every bloody one of them," he says. "Take your time, don't let them push you into a buy. Take your time."

Sure, will do. Three more days and we finally have it. A white fifteen-year-old Corolla with a validated number of 485,548 on the dashboard "odo". We have a tyre, oil and light bulb changed. That's always good to do before nailing down the cash. With a small daily limit on the card, we need two instalments: that is, two days to pay. No problem.

"You can borrow this old treasure and come back tomorrow with the balance."

Holden—the Australian version of Opel, Vauxhall or the uncreative GM—has this one last favour to do before inevitably falling apart. And miraculously, it lives up to it.

Meanwhile, sadly, our interim host loses it. We have come "home" late for the second time in a row and forgot to call. We "took our time"—too much of it—and he has an excellent solution. Why don't you disappear tomorrow? All of a sudden the car becomes a house. Not for long, however, because there is this next job we need to do.

9
Slowly, Slowly Catchee Possum

The right moment for the journey hasn't arrived yet. We are going north and ideally we need to start around June.

For the next few months we're going to house-sit a fibro cottage at the very fringe of Perth. And not just the house. We'll have a dog and three large cats to look after; not knowing whether we're minding them or they're minding us, it's an interesting experience.

The cats have different personalities. Tom Cat thinks he is a dog. Each time we go for a walk he is all for it. Fat Cat is asleep all day, with meal breaks in between. And Pocket Cat vanishes in the morning and returns at night with her stomach full of local fauna. The German Shepherd called Zsa Zsa barks in Hungarian because her owner comes from Budapest. Her husband, in turn, is from South Africa and he is fluent in German, English, Afrikaans and Zulu. One day he gave up, and like thousands of his countrymen, packed up and went to Australia. He brought and sold a yacht to get his money out of there.

So we now live in this house with no thermal insulation in

the walls and a bad one in the roof and fetch fresh raw kangaroo mince from a local farm outlet every day. The meat looks like salami—apparently the highest quality pet food in the world. The nearest bus stop is a good few kilometres away; we can't see the nearest neighbour, only his fence and his donkey, who goes by the name of Elvis.

Not all houses are like that, but in this one you can hardly breathe in the summer heat, and almost exhale steam in winter when the temperatures drop close to freezing. This somehow funny, flimsy, low budget, botched construction is quite common. Saving on utility bills is not exactly a popular sport yet.

There is a big ostrich farm nearby. An ostrich, unlike its Australian cousin, the emu, is an import from Africa. He is dumb. It's not a good idea to get too near. He can rip you open with his mighty claws—probably a dormant, intrinsic feat inherited from dinosaurs. One of his huge eggs equals twenty hens, and pancakes made of it are for the whole party of swearing bricklayers.

It is a strange feeling to be in this semi-seclusion. As if near a city, yet still far beyond. Only a few kilometres from here there is a new urban sprawl, and it's coming closer and closer every day, like plague. What were once inhospitable plains now belong to the fast-growing satellite towns behind tall soundproof barriers, with large shopping malls not far apart, reachable only by cars, wide streets and further infrastructure that in Perth is built systematically on huge budgets. There's also a small lake, at least on a local map. In reality it's an inaccessible muddy swamp with diverse vermin all around it.

The house roof gutters are full of redbacks—small spiders with a red dot on their backs—probably the most notorious leader of the arachnophobia charts. People like to mention redbacks to impress family and friends by saying how close to death they were when taking rubbish bins out on their holidays in Australia or after having one too many, as *Red Back* is also one of the local beer brands. With a little knowledge and prevention, the spider is harmless. Sweeping roof gutters with a broom, for instance, is a no-no because when they fall down to the ground, they can bite if stepped on. We walk in shoes, no matter how hot it is. And it *is* hot. Apparently, a tradie got bit on the willy by one the other day while reading a newspaper on a toilet seat, and there is even a song about it. In the song, his wife wants to help him with a knife but he objects the cure might be worse than the disease!

Western Australia has more mineral wealth than all the countries of Western Europe combined, and it is the de facto richest state. Some die-hard West Ozzies love to comment sarcastically, with a sizeable dose of patriotism and a visible sneer, "God bless the desert, separating us from the eastern states. We can do without them but they can't do without us."

Fremantle is a small town at the start of the Inner Harbour. Unlike the fast-growing city of Perth, Freo has European charm with low-pitched buildings and narrow streets. In one way, it's like the nearby Northbridge, a suburb, with better nightlife than in the Perth CBD, where after sunset everything clears out faster than a swimming pool with a Pollywaffle. Not that we want to know much about it now. We're in saving mode. We get up brutally early and the mere thought of it is keeping us awake, despite the fatigue.

Now and then a bird screeches so loud it might be taken for a human voice. A bloody murder just a few yards from our windows. With so many birds, a few kinds are squealing so loudly it can seriously damage the delicate ligaments of the permanently underslept nervous system. Once I even heard an imitation of my alarm clock coming back from the bush. Others, like the kookaburra—a large kingfisher type of a bird with a long beak—can laugh, in a truly hysterical chitter, and all you want to do in that moment is to kill it in cold blood.

As for other native animals, possums are noteworthy because they are a bit like a cross between squirrel and cat. The squirrelcats love to invade garbage bins, with quite some noise, and sometimes they come down from a tree at night, stop and stare into your torch without movement. Then they disappear in less than a second. While some of them are endangered protected rascals on Australian soil, no animal would possibly want to be a possum in New Zealand, where the only use they find for them are decorative furs.

Today we're getting up at quarter past two in the morning. We have to be there at three. It's the first cleaning shift. With eyes glued to the steamed morning window, I start driving towards the city in complete darkness. It's rather cold. The traffic lights at Freo intersection signals amber. Will I make it or not? At night it is often endless waiting: one car halted on red versus no traffic at all. Sure will. Except that the white Holden behind starts to strobe like a disco in the eighties. He immediately pulls me up.

In the rear-view mirror, I see a hulk of an officer getting out of his car.

"Good morning," I say, as if this wasn't going to provoke him even more. It's only five to three.

"Do you have driver's licence at all, mate?"

"Yes," I say and hand it out, saying nothing more. He takes it slowly and studies it patiently.

"This was issued in New South Wales," says the guy after a while.

"Yes."

He walks around the car, then returns.

"It wasn't amber, mate, it was red," he says slowly.

"I'm sorry. I was in a hurry," I say. I can't think of anything better.

Now I am only waiting for execution. *Coup de grâce*.

"Where are you going?" he asks.

"Work. Esplanade Hotel." New estimates start immediately to

feed my database of fines. It's not the first one.

"Mate. You'll go real slow now, never cross red again and have your driver's licence changed for the local one. Have a good day."

10
Pavlova

In 1929, one of the world's best-known prima ballerinas, Anna Pavlova, was on a tour around Australia. On her way home, after performances in the eastern states, she called in on Fremantle's Esplanade Hotel. She was exhausted. Australia had different rail gauges in each state and she'd had to carry her bags a few times from one train to another. She even carried a couple of birdcages with her.

She sailed to Perth this time and didn't forget about her little vice: a sweet tooth. Yes, strange. She was a ballerina. Despite being a world-class performer, in every port she visited, all around the world, she ordered sweet cakes. It was no different in Fremantle. The cook must have parted the previous night, only arriving in the small hours of the morning, tired. The slightest sound was like a heavy hammer pounding at his forehead. "Sweet cake for the ballerina."

"Sweet cake for the ballerina!" the special order stated.

"What cake?" he asked.

"Cake, cake," was the answer. "How am I supposed to know?" says the other voice in an insistent tone. "A cake. But quick. She doesn't have much time."

With his left hand supporting his heavy head, he reached for a bowl into which he instinctively threw a few egg whites. He added a pinch of salt and went on thinking about the previous night, while whipping, whipping and whipping, after which he started to pour sugar. The morning light from the window was entering his half-open eyes with an inverted image that was slowly being put back on its feet inside his brain.

"Come on, mate! Miss Pavlova is waiting," a voice demanded.

When he came to, the mixture of egg whites and sugar were a white, thick consistency. He added more *sugar*, vanilla *sugar*, *sugar* again and vinegar topped with *sugar*. Then he quickly chucked it in the oven. When it came out, he couldn't believe his eyes. He disguised the white pile with sweet fruits, the more the better, topping it with some whipped cream to fill the cracks.

A new recipe was born: Pavlova.

But of course, all that is a total and complete lie because the ballerina had had a similar experience in New Zealand around that time. So who does she belong to now? Nobody knows.

Sadly, she died young, only a few years later, but in a way, she lives on. Pavlova—the legend.

But enough cake. It's time to put our house in order and start packing.

11
Useful Tips and Off We Go

A car breakdown somewhere in the middle of nowhere can represent quite a serious problem if we don't have a professional logistical team of touring experts and a camera crew in tow. The former would quickly repair it and the latter would make it look like we fixed it ourselves. However, we're not a TV show. We are on our own.

There are many car wrecks along the long road stretches that didn't survive trips. Their once proud owners did not bother fixing or towing them, and left them behind like unwanted puppies after Christmas. Too expensive. Rusty, derelict, often burnt down vehicle torsos: that is the fate of cars that don't make it. It translates to

11 Useful Tips and Off We Go

the wallet as well. Get another car, new equipment, because everything had to be left a few hundred kilometres behind after somebody gracefully gave us a lift. Lucky there was enough space for the two of us and our toiletries bags. If something like that happens, incredibly large amount of time is lost. And what was to be a great adventure suddenly turns into unnecessary stress.

A well-prepared car is really important. At least in a few crucial points. Air conditioning should not be the main aspect when choosing it. There is a myth about Australia that it's hot, hot and hotter and you'll die if you don't fan yourself with cold air all day. When on the move, the open windows will do most of the time. On the contrary, it can be surprisingly cold. If money is an issue, invest in the engine rather than air con. Before setting out, it is critical that the engine has the cam belt—also known as the timing belt—changed. Not a cheap exercise but definitely worth it. If it the belt gives out on the road, we're only a little bit less than screwed. The repair will cost much more. A preventive change of the engine seal won't hurt either. It is highly recommended to check the oil level when the engine is cold before starting every morning. If the engine burns out, the car is a write-off and so is a significant part of our journey. The engine will often start in the morning and stop at sunset and when we open it, it will literally be boiling. So make sure the cooling system works. Tyres are another must. Go for good ones despite their price. The wear on our left GoodYear was significantly less than no-names we had to change a few times.

Have a good spare tyre and air pump, or the so-called "tyre seal" as a last resort. Petrol stations are every 100 to 200 kilometres, often more. If you go off the sealed roads, that distance gets longer and petrol gets more expensive. The further from civilisation, the dearer the fuel. Fuel stations in the outback are often in roadhouses, sometimes called homesteads, and they are grouped collections of buildings with a small grocery store and dust and flies hovering above.

If you use a tent, the size of the car is irrelevant. Organising things inside it, however, isn't. It's advisable to have a system, because after a month it will look exactly like the interior of a Russian tank in the final battles of the Second World War. The red dust is not such a problem as long as you know where things are. A knife or an opener or key disappearing somewhere down the trunk might mean hours of delay or worse, a toxic chain of events. For instance, in an attempt to make up for the time lost, we might forget to close the fuel tank and the lid—that rested on the roof—goes with you until you lose it in the roadside ditch many kilometres down the road. You won't buy a spare one in the next homestead. Junkyards and spare part stores will be thousands of kilometres away. It's also a good idea to have a second set of car keys. It sounds crazy, but a small distraction and a small mistake can turn your day into a nightmare.

We only used a spare fuel tank once. It is not as necessary as the drinking water canister; that must be topped up whenever possible. Before breaking camp each day, we get familiar with the road. We make each day's distances even and realistic.

Driving in Australia is tiring and so we allow for a lot of breaks. We take it easy. The kilometres ahead will not run away. It is a good idea to set off well after sunrise and stop well before sunset, avoiding driving at dawn and dusk. The omnipresent kangaroos love to go and check the road during that time. The risk of hitting them rises significantly. So let's say at 8 or 9 am we pack up and start, then in the afternoon, at about 4 to 5 pm, we start looking for a place to stay. There are many so-called rest places, rest areas or simply spots where one can stop without bothering anybody.

Town bookstores offer travel literature where we look the places up. There are many titles that provide detailed road breakdowns. We can either write them down or just buy the book. That investment will pay for itself in no time. We are after twenty-four-hour rest places that are free. But even if they're not marked as twenty-four hour, we can still stay overnight. Tiredness is our enemy and having a good rest is a priority. Nobody will chase us away if we're tired except overzealous rangers in popular national parks. That's rather rare. We will meet other "explorers" there—in cars big and small, in tents or caravans, on motorcycles or pushbikes, scooters, skateboards, on foot, in Trabbies, garbage bins, rolling on

11 Useful Tips and Off We Go

ping-pong balls, coin edges, razor blades, each one of them trying to make their mark on social media and establish hegemony in their niche loony categories, and even ordinary travellers.

If we happen to be there alone and the place looks dodgy, we wait a bit. If nobody shows up, we just go on to the next one—that is why we need to start looking early. They are usually about fifty kilometres apart. Birds of a feather flock together and most travellers get settled in about one to two hours before sunset.

Australian soil is often so hard you can hardly pitch the tent in it. Having a good hammer might be a good idea. Even if the ground is nice and soft, we haven't won yet. There are often grass thorns called bindies, and so good mattresses will also help. When I am relieving myself in the dark shrubs at night, I don't forget about cobwebs. Especially in the north, Golden Orb Spiders—a huge, hairy bugger—lives between tree limbs and in shrubs. Rubbing it off the face in a half-asleep mode isn't counted in any list of pleasures.

We always tighten the tent firmly to the ground or any solid structure. We might enjoy watching stars and contemplating a cloudless night, and still get blown away by heavy wind by the morning. In these modern times, phone cards are history and only God almighty—and Telstra, the omnipotent telecom—know what will become of the phone booths in the outback. There might still be some and if they're not jammed they might even work. Have some coins and cash on you. If not for the phone, you will need it to pay for bush camps and they don't take credit cards. Believe it or not, they don't have any ATMs on the spot either. These places are in the middle of nowhere. You're just asked to throw money in an envelope and leave it in a box, ready for the rangers to pick it up next day. Satellite phones? Now, that's ridiculous. Real explorers don't use those.

It is a good idea to have large plastic bags—the ones used for rubbish bins for different uses. In showers we wear *thongs*, well, those were already mentioned, almost to be a national emblem. Showers we encounter in the outback aren't exactly what we call five-star. Usually they are no stars at all and less. It doesn't take great imagination to picture what's going on in there.

And the last thing: we try not to lose our cool under any circumstances. Firmly screw your head to the rest of the body and keep it there all the time.

We're almost ready to go.

II. Perth to Broome

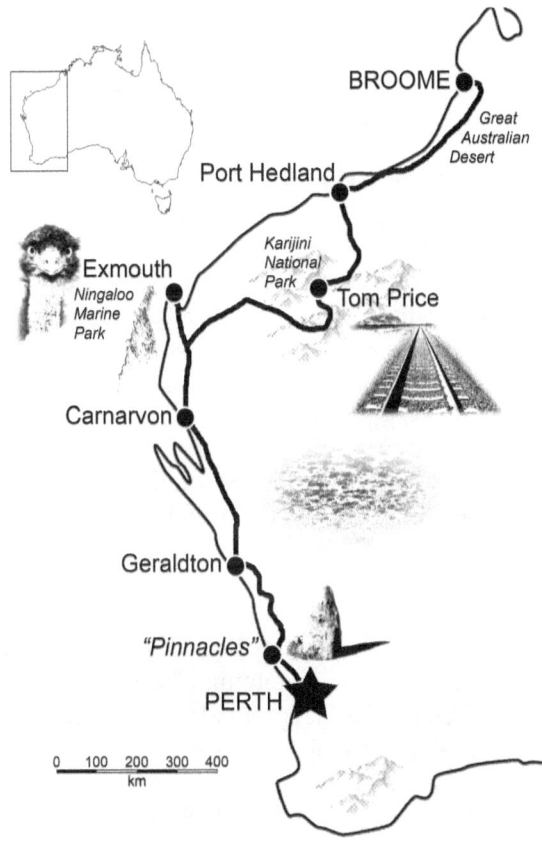

12
At the Bottom of the Sea: Pinnacles

"Don't trust everything you read. A map is a good thing but never mistake it for the terrain," says Eman, our eighty-seven-year-old friend, one night before starting off. He knows what he is talking about. He spent his life working for the Bata Shoe Company in different countries of the world like Kenya and Uganda, later India and Bangladesh, managing factories of a few thousand employees. He retired in Australia.

There are a few open travel guides on the table. The size of Australia hits home on a detailed map. It's comparable to the entire European continent from its very eastern fringes of Ural to Lisbon in the west. The nearer the mountain, the steeper it seems.

The distance can be felt right on the first stretch from Joondalup to the sandstone formation of Pinnacles in the Nambung National Park. The Brand Highway takes about three hours and doesn't have many overtaking lanes. For a good hour we are driving through a pine forest that is rather a huge tree plantation. But in Australia it can be anything else. The folks just learned to use the huge open spaces to yield something useful out of them and you occasionally come across them.

When we turn left off the highway called number one, in the western direction on Bibby Road, it is a long span going toward the ocean—a wide-open stretch.

The horizon shows itself a few times until the small town of Jurien Bay. There is white sand along the sides, but shortly before the iconic park it turns yellow. Nambung National Park[1] is not large but this one is like no other. It is better known as Pinnacles because there are these "pins" sticking out of the ground. Thousands.

When the first seafarers were exploring the Western coast of Australia around the year 1800 and earlier, they noticed strange formations—thousands of stiletto-shaped rocks strewn across a relatively large area, grandly sticking out of the yellow ground, often as high as three metres. Apparently they first reminded them of ruins, but only much later they realised they were purely natural. The formation made of limestone shells is a seabed gone dry. It's been exposed to sun, rain and wind for thousands of years.

---

1 The Pinnacles, WA http://goo.gl/maps/2qx6

12 At the Bottom of the Sea: Pinnacles

The Pinnacles: Nambung National Park

There is a tiny sandy road making its way around natural sculptures of different sizes and shapes. It is a one-way road. Yes, even national parks have them now. The area is just too large to be walked on foot. The sun lends the rock and sand exceptional colours. Pinnacles are iconic.

The evening sky in Jurien Bay looks promising. Another sunny day in sight, we think. It is very interesting how the land changes going north from there. Up to Geraldton there are dozens of large farms, thousands of acres of land with hundreds of cattle and even more sheep, huge green-and-yellow spaces, laced with dried out tree-tops, some of them a result of ring-barking —a technique used to clear land of lush trees: with a ring cut around their circumference, they will simply die without the need to cut them down. Easier. There are crosses along the road too—silent reminders that even an empty straight road can be treacherous. Very treacherous in fact because it lulls the senses to sleep and that is never good.

Every now and then we cross a cattle grid that is often marked with the yellow *Slow Down* road sign. Cows don't like to walk on uneven surfaces and so the grid serves a natural barrier, a kind of a fence in the ground.

Otherwise regular landscape, reminding us of Europe at times, is disturbed by *defects*—patches of land that refused to succumb to the agricultural obsession of the modern-day settlers, who tried to carve the landscape to their image. Those parts as if openly resisted and keep its wild and unkempt character. The further north, the more irregularities and the longer they are, until they become barren land entirely. Near Binnu, not far from Geraldton, farms are disappearing from sight and the dryness is getting the upper hand. Here somewhere the more isolated parts of Western Australia begin. There is a *Free Coffee for Driver* sign from time to time. It is a volunteer-run program to reduce fatigue-related accidents. It is certainly better to stop and sip coffee than be scraped off a tree at the nearest turn. Are you tired? Then don't wait. Stop! That's the message. The road starts to be very long indeed.

We stop at a twenty-four-hour rest place. There is a beautifully clear sky with thousands of stars in the evening. There are no lights around. What a fantastic weather we have got. Lucky us. Such an easy country to travel. That's exactly the moment we should have touched wood.

But we didn't.

13
Spider from Nerren Nerren

Nerren Nerren rest place is about 100 metres from the main road where heavy trucks roar all night. The place is among bushes and we have to set up the tent on a very hard gravel surface. There are wooden shelters. We tie our tent to one of them not knowing yet how wise this would later prove. In the middle of the night, strong gusts of wind wake us. They come and go, regularly returning each time we fall asleep. The wind gradually increases to the point that the tent canvas almost wraps around our bodies, then springs back to its shape. After the breathtaking Pinnacles, this is like a cold shower in the middle of the night. Which actually comes right after.

13 Spider from Nerren Nerren

In the morning a huge spider sits on the inside mesh of the tent. Rather crude awakening. It's about three inches wide and it's hairy. It was looking for a shelter and it's found one. Should we be concerned?

Huntsman spider on a tent mesh

It was a late night in 1981 in Sydney when Gordon Wheatley noticed a blown-out light bulb in the dining room. Time to go to bed but he's going to change it anyway. Setting up the ladder, he steps on something sharp. A bloody pin, he exhales to himself. But when he looks down, he is taken aback. He's just stepped on the most venomous spider in the world: *Atrax Robustus*, better known as the Sydney funnel-web spider. Only a year ago a child died from a similar bite. What followed were the most frightening several hours of his life. His nervous system went through a storm. His blood pressure doubled, his hands were cramped and his lungs started to shrink uncontrollably. Yellow substance came out of his mouth. The family took fifteen minutes to get him to the local hospital. Before they did, his skin had bluish spots and the blood pressure reading taken by the first doctor read 100 beats per minute. His lungs started to fill with water. He tore the mask off his face in convulsion; he was drowning in his own fluids. The local hospital was not prepared for that. He was taken to a bigger one. There, Dr Malcolm Fisher tells Mrs Whitley that her husband will be the first man in the world taking a newly-developed antibody. *If he agrees to it of course.* Not that he had any other choice. *Don't worry madam, it was well tested on chimps.*

Mr Whitley's heart was now on 155 beats per minute when the first antiserum entered his body. First dose: nothing. He was served another one. No improvement. Then the third one and no response at all. The patient was still in agony.

The doc picked up the phone and called his friend. Struan Sutherland had spent fifteen years of his life developing a vaccine. The development was sabotaged by bureaucrats, whose main job description was cutting public funds for research. Yet he managed to develop a highly specialised technique of milking spider venom. Now, at half past one in the morning, somebody was yelling at him that his antidote was good for nothing.

"The stuff doesn't work!" shouts the doctor on the other side. "This is the third dose now! What do I do?"

"Well, give him more, I suppose." The doc hangs up.

An hour later, the phone rings again.

"It doesn't work! What should I do now?"

A short silence.

"If that didn't kill him—give him some more. Some more."

Another hour and the phone rang for the last time.

The patient was improving. The famous antidote worked and the success rate is ninety-seven per cent. The breakthrough hit medical journals. Since that day, no other spider-inflicted fatality in Australia has been recorded.

But then, the funnel-web lives around Sydney only. An interesting peculiarity. As if this was nature's riposte for the city dwellers' pomp. We're in Western Australia now and have studied spiders rather carefully. What we're looking at now is a huntsman—a rather harmless and even useful creature, although he doesn't look that way. In fact, he looks like a crab, which is why he is also known as the giant crab spider. Most often you meet him sitting on the apartment walls every now and then. He likes posing for pictures and you can even place him in a plastic box and have him for a pet. He will dismantle cockroaches right in front of your eyes in the matter of minutes. Just don't kill him. He wouldn't kill you. He is a friend. We're packing the tent and he's walking off on his own.

14
Pouring Buckets: Monsoon Rain

Up until now we actually haven't known what a monsoon rain is. There is a drizzle in the morning. Nothing big. Surely it's going to stop as soon as we pack up. But it won't. It won't stop the whole day. It won't stop tomorrow, the day after tomorrow, not even after then. The road becomes monotonous. There are bushes all along; often you can't see what's behind them. Here and there the cattle grid sign comes in sight—*slow down*.

Typical road with a grid

There is a roadhouse every few hundred kilometres, which is a dusty building with a gas station next to it and a basic grocery store. The buildings are both somewhat rough and neat at the same time. There are travellers working in them—largely the work and holiday visa people from overseas.

A fresh wreck of an otherwise new-looking Toyota Prado is on its roof near the roadside, with all sorts of clobber and camping gear strewn around it. We stop and look for people. There are none. Something happened. Somebody must have given them a lift shortly before us. To hospital maybe?

With continuous rain, we notice the Floodway signs[2] for the first time. All of a sudden the flood poles along the road start to make sense as well. Flash floods they call them. Sometimes we see an occasional stream of water flowing across the road, otherwise large steady pools. Meanwhile the rain gets even thicker and there is no end in sight. One day after another. We put the tent up in rain, we pack it up in rain again. We eat in rain and go to pee in rain.

Floods at the Western Australian coast

The car is full of moisture, the heating is on full speed, the windshields are fogged. I can hardly see anything ahead. It's pounding and the sky is dark grey. The water pools get bigger and longer—now a few hundred metres each. Some of them have quite a strong current. Our car isn't built for that, that's for sure. The longest pool

---

2 A stretch of road with a Floodway sign, WA http://goo.gl/maps/7UMc2

so far had water level reaching just half-way up to the tyre top. It doesn't feel good. There are mighty 4WD's coming down from the other side—nothing of our hatchback sort that would give some comfort. The rain is unforgiving. The last water obstacle is right before the town of Carnarvon. It's longer and deeper. I am already thinking about what we'd do if the engine died right in the middle of it. Everybody is just happy to get the hell out of there, let alone to help some stuck losers. We have to push on. Being finally through it, we decide to stay in a caravan because by now we're completely soaked. But the mattress inside the caravan didn't escape the rain either. It's all wet from a leak in the roof and so there's only one other bed left. It's sticky, warm and humid. In the morning, we jump over all the pools leading to the Reception. In the local information centre they tell us that the road south, the one we arrived yesterday, is now officially closed. The road north, the one we need to take is still open, but flooded with long water patches. They don't recommend that we go but it's up to us. Carnarvon is a small town and apart from banana plantations there is little to see. We're going.

15
Sea to Mountains

We call our car mechanic in Perth. *How deep can we go with our small car?* It depends how high the engine air outlet is. About a foot should be all right. But there is one thing that can help, he says. Take a big rubbish bag and throw it over the front of the engine so that it hangs down and covers the registration plate. Close the bonnet over the bag and slowly go. It has to be a "constant and continuous drive with no stopping, so that water flows underneath the engine". We go across, slowly, patiently. The mechanic was probably just having a lend of us while answering an idiotic question, but it seemed to work. And maybe it was just pure luck.

Finally, the rain becomes less intense. We have to stop and dry. Near Coral Bay, we stop next to a caravan. The people invite us in. Jim and Anne come from New Zealand but live in Brisbane.

Their kids are living in their house while they're on the road. It's been two years now. They are retired and enjoy travel. It's a lifestyle thing. People even sell their houses and buy superbly equipped caravans.

The last water patch is slightly more daunting and looks like a creek. Then, as though by the wave of a magic wand, the rain stops at last. And although the heavy clouds remain, it's the first time in a week we can rest outside.

There are hundreds of strange-looking things to the left and right of the road that look like loads of something brown. Some of them small, some of them massive; they are everywhere. We're going to call them piles until we find out what they are.

North West Cape Peninsula is a promontory separated from the rest of Australia by Exmouth Gulf. The road is endless. Thanks to the local coral reef called Ningaloo Marine Park, it's a place for divers from all over Western Australia. The reef is not large, only about 280 kilometres, but it's unusually close to the shore, a miniature answer to the Great Barrier Reef in Queensland. It's an isolated place with one road wrapped around it—one that ends somewhere past the Cape Range National Park. Ideal for snorkelling, and when the season strikes from March to June, whale sharks, the largest living sea fish, arrive here and you can swim and dive with them. If you want.

In just about the middle of the peninsula, there is an interesting but closed area. Here be dragons—so to speak. An American Naval Communication Station is officially on the map not far from Exmouth, but apparently the whole place is a military playground nobody seems to know much about. It's a navy surveillance complex monitoring traffic in both the Indian and Pacific Oceans officially. Leaked information about its nuclear applications was all but shushed some time ago. It's situated ideally—on a landmass separated by both sea and ocean, on a hill, and it's got a lot of space to play with if needed where nobody will ever go. There are some narrow paths with *No Entry* signs from the main road.

Because of the small human population on the peninsula, there is a thriving animal habitat. Kangaroos roam freely, some of them quite large and so being cautious may pay off. An emu family is crossing the road and silhouettes of a few large wind turbines start appearing on the horizon.

Emu crossing the road near Exmouth

Cape Range National Park is just around the corner, not far after Exmouth[3]. We go uphill, towards Vlaming Head—a large lighthouse with a nice lookout. We are enjoying the slightly improved weather in the local caravan park, and kill time trying to fish on a small jetty. About a two-hour drive remains to reach the national park from the town. The jetty is rather fragile and something big is slowly swimming in the water near it so we're quickly out. The hefty dose of rain and strong gusts of wind at night don't bode well for the weather forecast, yet it improves the next day. Before long there is sun and we can stop at Yardie Creek[4]—a place to be, if we had a kayak or canoe.

---

3 Exmouth and North West Cape, WA https://goo.gl/maps/nVZHqMEyEjs
4 Yardie Creek, Cape Range National Park, WA https://goo.gl/maps/L9CdwFA-1JW62

Canoeing in Yardie Creek, WA

We don't have one, but never mind because we can admire wallabies from very close when strolling up the rocky gully upstream. They live here in perfect symbiosis with the surrounding brownish walls. They are the same colour and so are not easily spotted. Their jumping skill on the rocky surface is something to think about. Another traveller tells us the brown piles all around us are actually giant termite mounds.

The next stretch after leaving Exmouth will be long. We're driving inland to the local highlands. Tom Price is about 550 kilometres away. Cars are rather rare in these parts, and what's even more amazing is the calmness when stepping outside. We have to unblock our ears by swallowing and yawning, so quiet it is. 360 degrees of nothing. Every now and then a cow or a kangaroo crosses the road. The mild coastal air is becoming crisp, like that in the mountains. Hill tops start popping up near Paraburdoo, but they are different—reddish in colour. We are higher and higher above the sea. We need to push eighty more kilometres but it's getting dark. There is nothing between that little town and Tom Price. Only shrubs and rocks along the way, from which every moment a kangaroo might jump out and wreck the car. Seeing one during the day is not a problem. It's fast and vanishes quickly from sight. It is a confident creature. Often it stops and watches the car getting closer, only to jump out of the way at the last moment. Kangaroos don't have excellent sight, but thinking they are the fastest, they have quite a bad anticipation of speed—especially at night when the head lights might be a bit of a curiosity for them. They might even attract them, "Hey what's it there around the bush? Must be early sunrise! Let's check it out fellas!"

An average adult roo might easily weight eighty kilos—and so the impact on the car is significant. We monitor the roadside closely for any animal shapes. It's quite a strain on the eyes, especially after 500 kilometres or so. There are roaming cows too, but they are more intelligent and don't tempt fate so much. Plus they are slower. There is one more thing that plays against kangaroos. Unlike cats, their eyes don't reflect light and don't glow much when the light beams at them. These are our ponderings in the middle of a perfect pitch-dark night. And we don't know where we're staying tonight. The local backpackers' should be a perfect choice in preparation for the local unique colourful mountains.

16
Iron Prince of Pilbara: Tom Price

In 1952, a special guest paid a visit to the would-be town called Tom Price. Lang Hancock, an Australian billionaire and natural resource magnate, touched down in his private jet. He stepped out, and with the eye of an insider, he started to wonder about the beauty of the surrounding landscape. He bent down and scooped up a bit of the dirt that was everywhere around him, and caressed it gently. He let it fall through his fingers: *there*. What he held in his hands was top-quality iron ore. He was imagining giant trucks crisscrossing the local endless horizons, kilometre-long trains, mammoth-sized ships and industrial harbours that would take all that to the world markets. *Yeah*, he muttered again, walking back to his plane while shaking off the dust off his hands: *Let's get out of here.*

At that time Australia was under a government embargo on

iron ore, because the government didn't know if there was enough of the stuff to justify exports.

But Hancock knew. He was not hallucinating. His visions started to materialise in 1961 when the embargo was lifted and a new empire was born. From that time, Tom Price—the highest situated town in Western Australia at 747 metres above the sea—has been dubbed the Iron Crown of Pilbara. What used to be Hamersley Ranges is today officially called by its traditional name, Karijini, and it became a national park. Well, part of it anyway. Why would they call the town Tom Price? Thomas Moore Price was a vice-president of Kaiser Steel, which would make him—a client. *Oh, gentlemen, what a nice present!* Anyway, this guy was popular and even had "ore" built in his middle name, so why not. One way or another, the empire still exists. Conveniently tucked away from the curious eyes of most because not many people are bothered to get anywhere near this place.

It is here that other Australia begins. One that 500 million years ago used to be seabed and now looks as though it were ripped open with something sharp[5].

Giant cracks of Karijini, WA

Millions of years of the elements—water, fire, wind—have cre-

---

5 Giant cracks of Karijini, WA https://goo.gl/maps/GP83yNJU1GA2

ated spectacular gorges. To name it as one of the most beautiful places in Australia is no exaggeration. Layer after layer of different rock sediments make up walls that go deeper and deeper into the earth and narrow down into a red labyrinth of colourful hellish-like gullies.

We've been driving on that hard red dirt for about thirty kilometres and wonder if the road is going to be as bad all along. We are on Banjima Drive[6]—the approximately 100-kilometre and most interesting stretch that goes through the heart of the park. It's called unsealed or corrugated road and is made of stones of different sizes and grades, and also an endless number of parallel ridges only a few inches apart, which at times disappear completely, or intensify to such a degree that the steering wheel starts to shake uncontrollably until the very non-4WD Corolla slows down to about ten to twenty kilometres per hour. To see the most interesting places, we need to conquer about eighty kilometres on this road. It is worth it.

Banjima Drive: the road to gorges

---

6 Banjima Drive, dirt road to gorges, WA https://goo.gl/maps/QzcKgnwojiR2

II. Perth to Broome

17

The Nanny

In Australia, things simply work. There are signs everywhere: warnings, tags, announcements, notifications, leaflets. If a road is being fixed, it's clearly marked, signposted, and fenced. Two guys are sweating their arses off in a ditch, and three others (at least) are standing nearby holding stop signs in each direction like human sculptures all day long. Here is a special sign you can't do this, there is another sign you're not allowed to do that, here are other warnings that something else might happen to you if you don't comply. You see them everywhere. Often there are about twenty no-no's on one big board listing "can't do" stuff. Sometimes it might perhaps be easier and less costly for material to actually make signs with "can do" stuff. Common sense looked after most of those things in the olden days: when I slip on a bloody banana and break my leg, I can only put it down to my own stupidity. I should have looked better because it was right there in front of me! The modern approach is more from the common law realm: people are immediately invited to ask whose pavement and whose banana that was.

Some years ago a surfer got a massive payout from a council for breaking his neck against the sand because he was swimming in an area marked safe. That part of the beach was the council's domain, with life saver volunteers in place. He didn't know that swimming can sometimes be dangerous too, even between the flags. Another signpost needed, or just more common sense?

Once, I needed to buy a ninety-five per cent spirit for a health recipe, and I had to prove to the booze shop owner that I was not a nutter who was going to drink it straight, because an eighteen-year old had drunk shots of it and died some years ago and now they talk about banning it altogether. Again, more rules and pointing fingers, or more responsibility and common sense? Today's system of values increasingly likes to do the thinking part for the people to make up for their dwindling self-preservation instinct. A *nanny state* that tries to prevent everything before it happens. Plus peo-

17 The Nanny

ple love the blame game. If somebody damages somebody else's well-being, the latter is happily ready to sue the shit out of the former. If you neglect *duty of care*, you are in trouble.

This is also why nobody in his right senses will be very keen on informing you about places where you might hurt or kill yourself. No provider wants to become a sucker to this kind of a system, and so all the tourist tracks tend to be fenced, combed, made-up, nail-polished and hair-groomed. They play it safe. A bit unfortunate for a country with these tremendous possibilities, one might say, but what if common sense is really less and less prevalent in people these days? If too many tourists start falling down marked tracks, the company, the council, the state, or whoever is in charge will simply close it down. Not being able to discourage idiots becomes a costly business. It's not worth the risk and nobody takes chances. A lot of interesting places are disappearing from the maps and official guides this way. And there are more rules, precautions, rules and precautions.

*

Western Australia still seems to be a little bit more laid-back in that regard than the eastern states. An overseas tourist fell into one of the local gorges yesterday. The rescue crew arrived from Newman, about 250 kilometres away, and it took all day to pull the poor soul out of the narrow crevasse. We're encouraged to inform rangers where we're actually going. Some places are so remote and isolated that, if we're not careful and fall, who knows, after a few millennia, we might end-up rare stone imprints in a national museum, still holding the selfie stick and pushing that stupid smile.

The people who arrive here are inquisitive explorers with luxury of time, not the comfort seekers. If bitumen roads through the park are built one day and mainstream tourism hits the place, nobody knows how things will play out. Would the tracks be marked with *No Entry* or *Access with Guides Only* signs? Would Karijini become the second Uluru in a perfect "look but don't touch" reality?

We're trying to take it easy and enjoy the moment.

18
Walking On Ore: Karijini National Park

Karijini National Park was once known as Hamersley Ranges after Edward Hamersley—a rich early settler who made money on the colonial politics of land distribution. The place got back its traditional name only towards the end of the twentieth century.

Karijini boasts one of the largest deposits of iron ore in the world and the local hills are literally red in colour. It wouldn't be much of an overstatement to say you're actually walking on iron ore. When looking at the landscape from above, you can't help but thinking that somebody from somewhere up the celestial ladder has cut the earth with a giant knife. There are deep ravines and gorges, and you can look into some of them and actually walk them down too. First, however, you need to get to them by a rather bumpy road.

Inside one of the gorges of Karijini, WA

There are two roads to Karijini from the west—one from Tom Price and the second one from Paraburdoo. Both of them will merge into Karijini Drive[7], from which we need to turn to the bumpy Banjima Drive. After thirty kilometres or so we're finally at the gorges: Hancock Gorge, Joffre Gorge, Weano Gorge,

---

7 Railway crossing on Karijini Drive http://goo.gl/maps/djly

Red Gorge, Wittenoom Gorge, and Knox Gorge[8]. Sometimes it's a walk along steep walls, sometimes through narrow crevasses: local maps and guides rate them into several difficulty levels. The more interesting are fours, fives and sixes.

There is water at the bottom, either a fast-running stream or larger pools good enough for liloing—riding on inflatable mattresses. Cockatoos fly and rest inside the walls and they are fairly close sometimes. Handrail Pool is at the bottom of a chained path leading to a rocky enclosure. Weano Gorge is a starting point to get there.

Descending a gorge

Knox Gorge however is probably the best. Once we get down, the track is forking into two paths. The one to the right is a beautiful river surrounded by colourful rocks on both sides—a photographer's paradise. The shorter one on the left leads to a place where a huge boulder is stuck between opposing walls.

We can get on top of it but the stream underneath disappears suddenly and it is not clear how far and how deep. We are at the bottom of a narrow crevice balancing over a gushing stream of water.

---

8 Karijini Gorges https://goo.gl/maps/C63pJ22QPVm

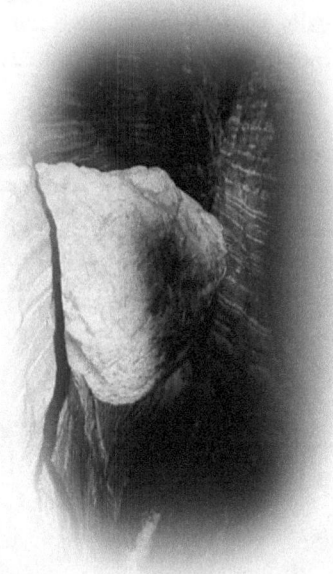

Boulder in Knox Gorge

Joffre Falls on the way back is a great swimming place. That's reserved for the next day though. We sleep in the Savannah campground.

The local aboriginal community is in charge of it. It's nice, clean, there is deafening silence at night and there is a bush shower—a very inventive one. Warm water from a large tank on the roof is tapped into a pouch with a nozzle, raised up on a rope; and we have two minutes of perfect water refresher.

The tourism industry is microscopic compared to the mining juggernaut. The area is mainly used by primary industries that gently scar the local landscape it in the name of economic growth.

The heavy weights aren't visible at first. The whole national park is cut in half by a narrow corridor, a train line which goes along about a 300-kilometre railway track from the giant open mine pit at the foot of Mount Bruce to an industrial harbour in Dampier.

Bush shower, Karijini, WA

The track is formally outside the national park boundaries and is used by extremely long trains. It's equipped with sensors so that somebody at a desk in a remote city office can monitor whether they're fit for millions of tonnes of iron ore rolling on them every day. To see the trains, though, in their full splendour, we need to walk up the second highest peak of Western Australia. Therefore, the whole next day is reserved for Mount Bruce.

Railway track near Mount Bruce / Punurrunha, WA

The first part of the nine-kilometre trek offers breath-taking views—a huge theatre stage on which two slow-moving two-kilometre long snake-like trains are passing each other—each of them having two large engines—in opposite directions. The empty train will be passing the full one for a good hour. We're counting the number of cars, stopping at 230 or so. The mine itself is still out of sight from this angle. We're sweating before getting to the top but the reward is great. Over two hundred carriages full of iron ore, up to 100 tonnes of it each. That's enough to make fifteen thousand cars, they say. Two-hundred tonne large capacity trucks that move forth and back look like small brown beetles. Where there is a giant hole in the ground today was once a mountain similar to the one we're standing on.

While the empty "snake" is ready to be loaded by the "beetles", the full one is already on its way to the Dampier shipping harbour—the largest of its kind in Australia. It had to be specially deepened for the fully loaded ships that would take fifty million tonnes of iron ore out to sea each year.

View from Mount Bruce / Punurrunha[9], 1,234 m ASL

9 Mount Bruce, Western Australia https://goo.gl/maps/FRifcB8hcPA2

Other peaks are visible from Mount Bruce: Mount Vigors, Mount King, Mount Frederick. We're a bit confused as to the name of the highest peak in Western Australia. Some said it was Mount Nameless / Jarndunmunha at 1,128 metres above the sea, accessible from Tom Price. But we're higher at 1,234 metres. Something's not adding up. Are we perhaps on the highest peak? No. Apparently Mount Nameless is the highest mountain accessible by car. Mount Bruce / Punurrunha is said to be second and the champion is Mount Meharry / Wirlbiwirlbi at 1,245 metres. The road to it goes through private land.

That night in the Dales Camping Area, we see dingoes for the first time. They wake us up in the middle of the night when they scavenge through the rubbish bins. The torch beam scares them and they quickly disappear into the darkness.

Nothing can beat Karijini from now on. At least that's what we think the next day, when it's time to leave.

19
Salt, Tibet And the Prophecy of Port Hedland

Karijini Drive—the only bitumen road across the national park—takes us away to the east and then north again to Port Hedland. It's true the landscape is nothing like the usual boring stuff we saw all around before coming here. The area is rocky, hilly and interesting. Auski Roadhouse is another service station in the middle of nowhere. Port Hedland is a dual-town, and no, it's not a spelling mistake. We stop at South Hedland, the more populated part. The Port is exactly what is says: the port. There is another giant train arriving—this time full of salt. It's produced here by solar evaporation and the few facilities make eight million tonnes or so of it, in excellent quality for export, through the same port used for the iron ore.

A bunch of local Aboriginal guys are drinking wine from goon bags in a shady part of the park, a huge rusty industrial facility in their backdrop. It's very hot, the town is empty and there is nothing else to do.

Industrial backdrop in Port Hedland

Two people in the local camp are about to make our day. One of them is in the course of crossing Australia on a pushbike, the other one is a prophet.

"I've come from Melbourne, heading for Melbourne," says the former.

Brian is the first of the army of cyclists crossing the continent. He's been on the road for two years now. We're going to meet more of those. Brian is touring Australia with the goal to help children of Tibet. When he was in Tibet, he happened to snoop in some unofficial places and he stumbled across a guy on the local market who handed him a scrap of paper with "Help children of Tibet" on it.

"You know," he explains with some irritation in his voice, "in Tibet, you can't go wherever you want to, they'll give you a guide who is going to be Chinese—guaranteed! They will show you what the government wants you to see. Poverty is not to be part of that picture. China is forcing its will on it and the world turns a blind eye. People flee to India, lots of children live in terrible conditions with little prospect of a future." Brian is a volunteer of an Adelaide-based organisation trying to financially help them. "The Australian government is doing next to nothing about human rights in China. There is just a lot of trade going on, and no matter who is behind the steering wheel, they just don't have the guts to touch it."

"As for sponsoring, you pick a case, a child that interests you, and you pay for school, food, et cetera as one-off or for a longer time. Even one dollar a day is a great help." Brian met the prime minister the other day but he didn't have any nice words for him. While on the road, schools help him a lot. They provide rooms for lectures, access to photocopiers, internet. He plans to finish his journey on Human Rights Day.

He has modified his bike for long-distance rides. He pulls a bob trailer behind him with necessary minimum of spare parts and tools. The less, the better. A miniature tent that just fits a miniature stove. Miniature everything.

"If you want to go around Australia on a bike, you need to read books by those who've done it before like Paul Elwood. The biggest problem is water. It weighs and seems heavier every new kilometre. And even though you know the water sources on the way, at some places there is no water at all, meaning, you need to carry sixteen litres of it sometimes." That's not a very comfy proposition. There is a spot in the Kimberleys with water only because a guy made a rest place on his private land there. They say his son got killed in a car accident and he wanted to remember him that way.

"And what are you doing here?" we ask a woman standing next to him. "I am touring around Australia. My engine blew up." I am waiting for a new one I ordered. I went three thousand kilometres and I didn't check the oil," she says calmly."Yeah, check your oil if you can. Don't end up like me. Each morning before setting out. It costs me more than the whole car".

The stretch from Port Hedland to Broome is 600 kilometres through a long edge of a desert with one stop only approximately in the middle—the Sandfire Roadhouse[10]. The desert on that side

---

10 Sandfire Roadhouse on Great Northern Highway, WA http://goo.gl/maps/AE7A

doesn't actually look like a desert at all: it's more of a wasteland with combination of scrub and sand on both sides. You can even see cows at the side of the road sometimes.

We plan to make it in one day and are ready: supplies, water, checking tyres, petrol. We're already driving when we remember the words from yesterday. The engine oil. On opening the hood, I can't believe my eyes. The engine is splattered with grease. There is a massive leak through a broken seal. Luckily, we're not far from the town and quickly turn for the nearest service station. The repair is nothing compared to what would have happened if we discovered it later in the day. That would be end. The woman was sent by heaven.

20
Great Sandy Desert

The Sandfire Roadhouse, in the middle of the Great Sandy Desert, where we sleep tonight, in between Port Hedland and Broome, is lush greenery that looks more like a zoo than desert. Thousands of small insects in the shower are prepared to ambush anyone who is foolhardy enough to put the light on. A large green frog sits glued to the window wall next to the toilet seat.

Australia is said to have made three historically significant mistakes: the first was the stolen generation, the second one was sending soldiers into the WWI and the third was the cane toad—the so called *Bufo Marinus*. They introduced it as a "natural" protection of sugar cane against pests. In short, it was to eat anything that eats the sugar cane. And it did. Except the toad took the initiative to a different level. It downed literally everything it could get its tongue on, alive or dead (it made little difference), and that created a mishmash in its stomach so toxic that every animal further up the feeding chain was faced with agonising death by poisoning. Between 1935 and 1980, the toad infested the whole north-east of the country, and if it weren't for the desert, it would be here too. It's clear this one is a harmless frog.

20 Great Sandy Desert

Harmless frog at Sandfire Roadhouse's showers, WA

We nicely put the tent up under a tall tree. The sky is perfectly clear in the morning but the tent is wet, as though it had rained heavily overnight.

"That's not rain, that's a hundred per cent humidity," says somebody from the neighbouring tent on the left.

"The tree has peed on you during the night."

A group of young girls came in an old car like ours and they now sit and sip their morning coffees next to the tent on the right.

"Condensation."

They've just got up while we're almost ready to go. This will turn against them that very evening. The sun dries the tent within minutes. We set out to finish the remaining 300 kilometres or so of the unbelievably straight *desert* road. All we can see is shrubs and flat land. Hours of it on both sides. This is what one and the only road from the south to the town of Broome looks like.

Many expeditions have scoured this part of the coast since the eighteenth century, and they started to systematically record their findings about the new mysterious continent in the south seas. The sources of the time were in no mood to suggest that one day (or ever) any European settler would feel like setting foot on something so inhospitable, let alone trying to settle or colonise it. Still back in 1803 the French explorer Commodore Nicholas Baudin and later Louis de Freycinet reported that:

> *The coast from the moment we saw it exhibited nothing but a picture of desolation; no rivulet consoled the eye, no tree attracted it; no mountain gave variety to the landscape, no dwelling enlivened it. Everywhere reigned sterility and death.*[11]

So much for the French.

The British colonial interests only bothered to take the west coast more seriously later and that mainly because of prospecting new pastoral land, and also because of excess of rotting boats full of prisoners on the Thames.

On arrival at the intersection to Broome, we know for sure we're in the tropics. One stop at a petrol station and we're sweating like pigs. The absence of the aircon is not the problem, but you need to be on the move. If you stop, you feel it. Not long after we're in Broome, a town they don't write much about these days. For somebody who has no clue about what happened here in the past, the town might look nothing much like a jewel. Tourism is the industry of the day and the beaches and caravan parks are chock-a-block. Night-life in the centre looks busy. There are backpackers, tourists, locals. An aboriginal woman is trying to pour boxed wine into a two litre plastic bottle. She is sitting on the ground and her hands are shaking so much that most of it ends up on the pavement. Larger four-litre *goon* is not on sale here. Unostentatious Broome has written history twice, with the first event being tightly connected to the second. From about the middle of the nineteenth century, mother-of-pearl was collected here (eighty per cent of the whole world's production at one stage) and then—although not many are keen to let it on and write about it—it staged one of the most blood-soaked chapters of the British colonisation of Australia.

---

[11] Jas. S. Battye, The History of the North West of Australia. Perth, 1915, p. 8.

21
Indigenous versus Mainstream: Take II

When the famous buccaneer William Dampier with his bunch of mates were circling the west coast of Australia in 1688 and circumstances forced him to take a maintenance break, he recorded in his diary while his crew was fixing his Cygnet:

The inhabitants of this country are the miserablest people in the world. The Hottentots, though a nasty people, yet for wealth are gentlemen to these; who have no houses and skin garments, sheep, poultry, and fruits of the earth, ostrich eggs and so on, as the Hottentots have. And setting aside their human shape, they differ but little from brutes. They are tall, straight-bodied, and thin with small, long limbs. They have great heads, round foreheads, and great brows. Their eyelids are always half-closed, to keep the flies out of their eyes, they being so troublesome here, that no fanning will keep them from coming to one's face ... so that from their infancy being thus annoyed with these insects, they do never open their eyes as other people: and therefore they cannot see far, unless they hold up their heads, as if they were looking at somewhat over them.[12]

The British did treat them as such. At that time until the beginning of the twentieth century, the papers were full of scientific essays about the genetic supremacy of the white race. The natives were regarded as bludgers and lazy-bones, who quickly and willingly adopted from the civilisation all the "good stuff", such as cigarettes or alcohol, but the "bad stuff", like work, was not their thing. To be more precise, work didn't apply to them at all, because material gain had no place in their culture. They interpreted life by spiritualism based on stories about animals, trees, caves, and so on and lived only on what they needed, mainly bush tucker. For the new landlords, this counted as a clear evidence that what they have to suffer on their newly acquired lands were a bunch of idling loafers: *they were at least going to work in stables and collect the pretty*

---
12 William Dampier, Dampier's Voyages, E. Grant Richardson, London, vol. 1, 1906, pp. 453-54

white little balls that grow in the sea. And categorically no money! They'd only spend it on booze!

Already, around 1880, the business went quite well. The pretty white little balls in the sea were aplenty, and before the natives gathered them up around the shores of Broome, the monarchy started to indulge in a new and lucrative trade—mother-of-pearl. Now they had to go deeper into the sea. Those who better mastered that skill, came out on top. Or to put it more bluntly—whoever had people who would do it for him—was coming out on top.

What happened to Aboriginal people in Broome is a very good representation of what was happening to them all around the country. The Aborigines could hardly defend themselves. Even if somebody cared, in those times a piece of news took months to even get out of the country. This was a totally isolated place, a remote outpost of the empire, that only a relatively few had access to. The colonies were not quick to let out anything that would compromise the interests of the monarchy. The world at that time had enough other problems.

The curiosity and interest of natives in their new visitors didn't last long. The first contacts were friendly, but when everybody went about their usual business, the old and new worlds proved to be incompatible. After a short indifference, the relations quickly deteriorated and then the colonisers took over and completely annihilated everything around them. The aboriginal defence was based on loud exclamations as a proof they were not afraid of the enemy. Their visible parades in the first encounters only made it easier for the other side to take better aim of their targets. They were badly outnumbered, and without firearms.

When the colonial might was handing out the land, its inhabitants became property of the new masters. Later, even *half casts*—how those of mixed parentage were called—could be dragged into forced education any time. Between 1900 and 1970, there were whole stolen generations of children who had been taken from their homes and placed in institutions. About fifty thousand or so. There were times when the British colonies differed from the

21 Indigenous versus Mainstream: Take II

American slavery system only in the fact that the British didn't have to import their slaves.

Farmers around Broome quickly understood that cattle was not going to make them rich. Looking after herds was hard strenuous work, the Aborigines were still spearing their cows, making the pastoralists even more furious, and the Kimberley Range was too hard a barrier to cross. So when the news of a new commodity broke out, all kinds of greedy rabble were arriving: from ex-cons through to unfulfilled bureaucrats sick of cities, to miners and gold diggers who couldn't sustain families. Having thirty or forty Aborigines working on boats for a few days could equal an average yearly income for next to no effort.

"You were not at the bottom!", yells the master. "Next time you go down, you present a bedrock! And shut up! No talking!" If one of them tried to reach for the boat, they were hit across their fingers. It wasn't rare even for a pregnant women to be forced to dive.

And we're talking going deeper and deeper. Bleeding nose was no excuse, some of them were getting strange pain in their arms, others lost consciousness or died unexpectedly. They didn't know about the bends or the decompression disease in those times. The dead stayed in the sea or were buried in the sand, right above the high tide mark. There were some who swam away, trying to escape. The master knew they didn't stand a chance.

The brutality had gone on to such a degree that in 1873 the government ruled no more women and children would be employed on the boats. The labour was hiding, of course, and so "recruitment" expeditions were organised. The market for blacks was thriving because no white man could be talked into working in such outrageous conditions. For any money. The slaves were taken off by force or voluntarily handed over and sold for a bit of food or drink by their own. Capturing or shooting an *Abo* had a tariff price. Five pounds. If they tried to resist, they were brutally punished. Often they were seized with "witnesses"—typically their women, who were chained to boab trees and repeatedly raped in front of their men. If a white settler lost his life during those expeditions by hand of any of the natives, a popular punishment was to tie the guilty one by his neck on a noose and drag him behind a horse through needle-sharp spinifex.

I don't want the town to be named after me, protested the governor of Western Australia, Sir Frederick Napier Broome. *It's going to be a ghost town soon,* he complained. Too late. The name had already been set in the printers. And it didn't become a ghost town either. The pearl industry grew and modernised. From 1880, special equipment was necessary to go even deeper and the local Aborigines were no longer in demand.

After about two decades of their intensive ruthless exploitation, hundreds of new settlers made fortunes. Nothing was left for the natives. Quite the contrary: with ruined health, alcohol addiction, and newly imported diseases, they were cast aside for a slow, agonising death.

And that's how Broome was born. A town with an amazing but unbelievably brutal past, so typical throughout the country. Nobody seems to be too quick to acknowledge that this was the very base of the newly creating state.

22
Tourist Broome

We pay for the last available spot at the Mango Camping Area. The three girls we met at the Sandfire Roadhouse didn't make it on time. There is only one road from Broome after all, and we meet the same travellers.

Broome has relatively wide streets with palm and banana trees alongside. The local jetty, hundreds of metres long, sticks out into the sea and is impressive. Fishermen are all around it.

A mighty boab tree near Broome, WA

In 1912—in the same year the Titanic sank—a steamboat arrived here from Perth, with twelve Royal Navy divers on board. They arrived because one year earlier a law had been introduced preventing the pearl boat owners hiring non-white crews. We're in the middle of the White Australia policy—the times of the British cultural hegemony. At that time about half of Broome was in Asian hands. Large Chinese and Japanese quarters powered most of the town's economy and the government lost its cool. The pearling industry here was mainly controlled by the Japanese. They stood out with their incredible diligence, discipline and hard work, and managed to have the upper hand, not only in the pearl business but also a significant influence on the social life of the town. They built a hospital of their own and the Japanese doctor was held in higher regard than the local one. There is an interesting theory about why there were so many Japanese.

A bunch of frustrated guys from Wakayama province is said to have walked through Melbourne during the famous Melbourne Cup in 1890. For a good few years they had been struggling to establish a decent living in Australia. The Melbourne Cup is sort of a national holiday. The few minutes of the horse race can bring the whole country to a halt as everybody checks their favourites. The boys checked theirs too and it was their lucky day. They'd won 22,500 pounds, which at an average yearly wage of about 100 pounds was a mind-bending sum. What are we going to do with it now, they thought? And so they invested in a fleet of boats in Broome—a town somewhere in the north-east of the country where rumours were going around of quick easy riches made out of the sea, but nobody wanted to say a thing. Wakayama had since been full of stories of easy pickings in Western Australia. Thousands followed in the next few years. Their advanced organisational skills, tenacity and their will to work for less than the locals gave them a huge lead.

And that's also why the Crown was going out of its way to prove once and for all it could do without the Asian mobs. And so the specially trained divers were able to dive for pearls with the same efficiency and vigour as the Asians.

The boys, however, were different kind of professionals—mainly helping in bridge construction or salvaging shipwrecks. They mostly worked in the murky waters of England and they were deployed in one-off operations. While having to stick to strict standards back at home, where they already knew much about the health implications of diving, their new employers in Australia took the divers' charts for less than bullshit. That was only hampering higher productivity and they could otherwise employ an Asian for three times less money. With the exorbitant wage rates paid to them, and the extra hours of surfacing, they were coming across as nothing but lazy whingers. Within a year, though, one of them was dead and two others were permanently paralysed. It didn't work.

Nobody knows today how many non-white divers died. The Asians were treated as foreigners despite being born in Australia, and the Aborigines have been counted as Australians only since 1971.

22 Tourist Broome

Being at the Japanese Cemetery[13] in Broome and walking between the rows of graves is like breathing history. About a thousand gravestones are silent witness to times gone by. The names engraved in their language are largely of people who died very young—killed by pressure-inflicted injuries and other diseases the medicine of the time knew little about.

Japanese Cemetery in Broome, WA: Katsujiro Maekawa, died at the age of 26.

Today the Japanese are arriving in the town in coaches and within their fourteen-day holiday span: already having seen the complete Australian east coast, including Sydney and Melbourne, they come to spend a few hours in Broome, before finally departing for Darwin for the final days of their trips.

They are now enjoying the town on which they had such a tremendous influence. They are so well-mannered that whenever their tourist guides inadvertently mention something about bombing this place by kamikazes during WWII, apologetic voices can be heard at the back of the coach, "sorry, sorry, sorry".

At one particular place in Broome, a tourist sign points to a spot where dinosaur traces are to be seen.

---
13 Japanese Cemetery in Broome http://goo.gl/maps/8JAl

We are going there. The spot, however, is three metres in water it turns out, because of the high tide, and all we can see is an information board. There is an incredible eleven-metre difference between low and high tides in Broome. Moreover, the dinosaur footprints are just cast in concrete. The originals, apparently—120 million years old or so—were stolen in 1997 by a network of international thieves. They were to be one of the few clear pieces of evidence at the time of dinosaurs having lived in Australia.

But the sunset here is really enthralling. The light reflected from the sea is said to create an optical illusion of a staircase gently rising to the very fringe of the full moon.

The overcrowded camp's tent section is young and busy. The caravan section is more settled, comfortable and cosy. The blinking lights are giving away TV screens; there are refrigerators, living rooms, kitchen cupboards, steaks are being prepared on hundred-kilo barbecue sets. Just why those people have to tow half their households on holidays with them remains a mystery. They probably want to live here, if only for a few days. It must be the smooth long beach—the incredibly flat, vast, unmatched elsewhere—the beautiful unforgettable beach.

These thoughts are slowly drifting us away deeper and deeper into sleep after fourteens days, about three and a half thousand kilometres, and with about twelve thousand more to go.

III. Broome to Darwin

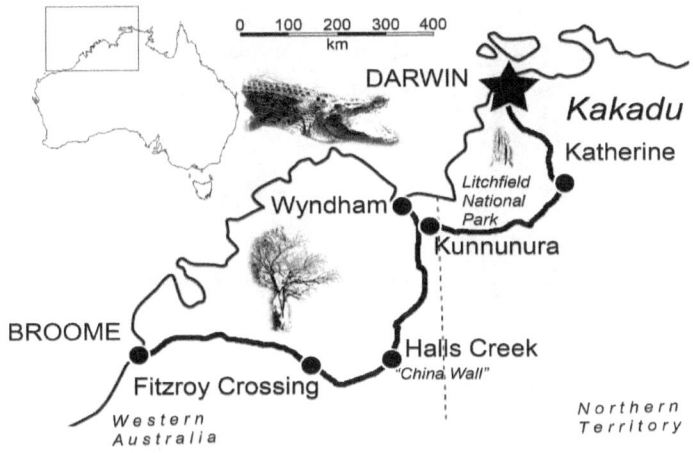

23
"That Funny Hotel": From Fitzroy to Halls

We check the engine oil this time. Willare Bridge Roadhouse is about two hours away from Broome. A signpost is showing distances to nearest places. The next one is Fitzroy Crossing, 230 kilometres away, then Darwin, 1709 kilometres. While still in Perth, about two weeks ago, a friend of ours happened to mention in a between the lines kind of way: "When you get to Fitzroy Crossing, don't be scared by the hotel." When we asked what he meant by that, he said with a bit of a malicious smile, "You will see."

III. Broome to Darwin

Distances from Willare Bridge Roadhouse, WA

Shortly before Fitzroy Crossing there is a left turn to Leopold Downs Road, a dirt road, which would go for about hundred bumpy kilometres and then turn into Gibb River Road. A well-known place called Tunnel Creek is not far from here on that road, and about thirty kilometres after that another called Windjana Gorge. Both are miniature national parks. Tunnel Creek is an entry point to an extensive tunnel system, good to be explored with a torch. It was here in 1897 when Jandamarra—a *terrorist* in today's official doublespeak but always a hero to the natives—was shot to death. He was one of the very few Aboriginal rebels who openly stood up against the increasingly expansive settlers and was too elusive to be caught by them in his natural environment. The British had to recruit one of his own to get him. Apparently the authorities had been so jubilant about this that they celebrated it by cutting his head off and sending it to London in a jar as a marketing souvenir. Fresh-water crocodiles might live there, which lends those places an even more eerie feel.

After about five kilometres into the dirt road we stop at a flooded stretch that isn't looking any good. You either go ahead or turn around. There is no other way. Go or not to go? That is the question. Al old Ford Falcon soon arrives from the other direction and faces the same problem. An Anglo-German-Dutch squad of three backpackers. It turns out these large pools are quite frequent on this rough road and might pose too big a challenge for a conventional car like ours. Their Ford's clearance is substantially higher though, yet it has to work really hard. Too much of a risk. We join them at the campground in Fitzroy.

The large number of houses on metal poles around Fitzroy surprise us. Apparently, the reason for this is twofold. One, there are termites virtually everywhere and they would chew the house from its base up to the top in the matter of days. And second, there are floods almost every year. The town was founded at a crossroad, a source of drinking water and a refuge from floods.

A truly historic hotel with a large terrace is said to be the oldest accommodation facility in the Kimberleys, dating from 1897. A small local information centre is quiet.

"Fitzroy Crossing has two campgrounds: Tarunda before the river and Fitzroy River Lodge after the bridge. Both are *safe*, even the one before the river is fenced," says an employee of the centre with a motherly smile.

"Why shouldn't it be safe?" we ask.

"You know. Today is a payday. You'll see."

The first smaller Tarunda campground is actually like a car park with a high fence around it. Spots are available but it's time to make a little trip around the town. A thick smoke can be seen in the distance. Back-burning, a way to control the bush—it's better to burn it a little by little at the right time than do nothing and wait for a disaster. A regular thing. The trick is to burn the tops without damaging the tree roots. Now, in close proximity to the road, a blazing three-metre-high flame is ruthlessly lashing any dry grass that stands in its way. We are trying to get back to the main road somehow and over the bridge to the other camp, and we pass simple houses where locals live.

Back-burning

A pub called Crossing Inn appears right after, and there are about twenty Aboriginal locals lying on the ground in front of it. They're enjoying their payday. A bit of a binge. A few heads are turning slowly as we pass them by. We have to drive carefully so as not to run over some of them. They are stretched all over. A pheasant-like bird with an extremely long tail is making a strange dance across the road not far from them.

Harry is an English backpacker who arrived here with a Work and Holiday visa, a status many Western countries enjoy in Australia, and a good idea too because it saves loads of money. You're allowed to work full time and earn enough cash to travel afterwards. Not a dumb system for Australia either because what you earn will stay in the country and support its economy. Many regional areas suffer from staff shortages and backpackers fill the gaps. Limited time is the downside. Many travellers arrive as students, on a status that except of being a bit of a rip-off—most colleges for international student are not worth the money—makes it very hard for them to leave a chosen city for more than a few days at a time, and also limits weekly working hours. Not meeting certain school attendance requirements means an automatic *adios*. The only other real alternative for any hope of a longer expedition is permanent residency, and this is not easy to come by. It's a long and painful assessment process that can discourage even the most patient individuals. The scoring system requires you to get enough points to match the profession and skill list, something that changes constantly according to Australia's current market demand, to prove the person's education from home and from Australia if it is finished successfully; it assesses your age category, work experience, the appropriate level of English, health condition, partner relations, that you are of good character, and so on and so forth. That's when all sorts of vultures descend on your bony skeleton to assist you in your quest to fulfil all the requirements Education agents skimming hefty commissions directly from schools so it looks like they do it for you out of sheer love, solicitors charging non-trivial fees for putting the paperwork together, plus other substantial fees for medical examinations, professional bodies certifications, language preparation courses and testing, proving clean criminal records from overseas and Australia, verifying the de facto relationship if one has a partner, and finding all the other smaller bits of the M. C. Escher's *Salita e Discesa* thousand-part jigsaw puzzle masterpiece, before you can submit the complete picture. Besides, the whole system constantly changes with the mood of those who are currently at the political steering wheel.

Work and Holiday is easier.

Harry's working phase is now safely behind him and he can concentrate on travels. His first job started exactly five months ago in Darwin. The advertisement was looking for kitchen staff and the owner was to pick him up at an agreed spot. A funny-looking pair, husband and wife, arrived to pick Harry up in a worn-down 4WD wrapped in red dust from tyres to the roof. It had an antenna on the front hood that was so high its upper end was getting lost in the sky.

The bearded guy didn't say much and neither did his wife. Short hello and off they went. They went for an hour, two, three hours, and the people didn't drop a single word. When it got dark and they hit a serious dirt road for the first time, Harry went a little edgy. He didn't want to tease his boss by impertinent questions right at the start, so he only casually remarked that he had never driven that far in his entire life and he was dying to see it on a map. Boss calmly replied he didn't have one and they would soon be there anyway. And that was it. A five-hour conversation. Harry was peeling potatoes the following few months but had he disappeared, he wouldn't have been the first. Harry knew something I didn't.

24
Vanishing Tourists Business

Ivan Milat is probably one of the front-runners on the list of well-known psychopaths. It looks as though he made killing innocent backpackers into his pastime, but not everything was as clear as it seemed. They proved seven murders by him.

On the January 25, 1990, an English hitchhiker by the name of Paul Onions decided to thumb a ride from Sydney. The guy who stopped was fine for an hour or so, then he turned weird and threatened to tie him up. Onions saw the rope and gun and after some commotion somehow managed to get the better of him, only just escaping in an oncoming car. He reported the incident and soon left the country.

In 1992 and not far from the same place, the remains of two women were found, later identified as missing British tourists. Both of them had strange incision marks around their spines, as if having been paralysed before death. Both girls' flies were unzipped. One had four bullets in her head. There was a small makeshift fireplace nearby. However, both victims were in such an advanced decomposition that not much could be established. Police denied any serial killer suspicion and continued a detailed and painstakingly slow investigation, including analyses of all cases of disappearance in the last ten years. A psychologist was employed in an attempt to decipher a mental picture of the possible maniac.

In 1993, more victims—this time an Australian couple—were found. They had disappeared in 1989. They had similarly unzipped trousers and a similar wound on the spines. A fireplace was also present. Police carried out a detailed search of the surrounding forest. Three days later, the last victims were found—a German couple missing from 1991. Ballistic fingerprints matched the ones previously discovered. One of the victims was without a head. and it was later suspected that skulls were used as targets. Police were now conceding for the first time that a serial killer could be involved. In 1994, the case was heavily promoted in the media, but that led to no significant progress until Paul Onions came back to Australia as a witness. His claim of having escaped a certain violent individual was confirmed by a woman, the driver of the car, who took him to a police station. If Onions recognised Milat, a warrant could be issued for his arrest, and that's what happened. A search of his numerous properties later revealed many artefacts belonging to the victims, and it also yielded the notorious weapon.

The trial started in 1996, and after a short time Milat sacked his defence lawyer because he had advised him to plead guilty. During his time in court, he vehemently denied any participation in the crimes, and some facts were actually playing for him. Firstly, he was a non-smoker and didn't drink, but there were large numbers of cigarette butts and empty bottles. Some of the evidence suggested that his family could be complicit, and that there were many more victims. Milat's fired defending lawyer, John Marsden, was to reveal before his death that he strongly suspected Milat had been helped by his sister. Later in 2007, evidence was sent to Britain for DNA tests on some of the items because the technology had not been available at the time of crimes. They were, however, not enough to charge anybody else.

After a fifteen-week trial, Milat was sentenced to six years for assault on Paul Onions and seven consecutive life sentences: one for each victim. He is doing his time in Goulburn Jail—one of the toughest places in Australia, with maximum security and bleak white clinical walls. All of his appeals against the sentence were rejected. Whenever he was asked about his crimes, he swore his innocence. He even swallowed metal objects to attract attention, and in 2009 he is said to have cut his finger with a plastic knife and wanted the case to be sent to the highest court.

"I don't miss my family so much. I miss my cat," says Harry suddenly.

"I can't send him an email."

25
United We Fall

The small national park called Geiki Gorge lies not even twenty-six kilometres from the town of Fitzroy Crossing. An English explorer, Sir Archibald Geiki, prospected this area back in 1883 and he was the first white in this place. The walls of the local information centre show watermarks—that's how high the water level is during floods. The highest one is right under the roof. In the wet season, floods can easily raise the water level by ten metres and spread sixteen kilometres away. The town can be cut off from the rest of the world for up to a month.

Geiki Gorge is a beautiful riverbed surrounded by massive rock formations and walking along its sand banks can be hard. There are flies everywhere and it's incredibly hot. The watermarks can be seen on the rock walls and not far from them, right in the middle of the river, a fresh-water crocodile is enjoying a sunbath. He might be about fifty metres away and doesn't let anybody disturb him.

Geiki Gorge, WA: River, crocodile, and rock wall

25 United We Fall

We meet the English-Dutch-German trio of backpackers in Halls Creek again which to our eyes is a carbon copy of Fitzroy Crossing. It's a small transit town with a significant population of Aboriginal people.

The information centre offers discounts on plane tours of the nearby Bungle Bungle National Park, also known as Purnululu. Two is a company, three is a crowd. They require three people at least to make it happen and that's where the European "alliance and solidarity" manifests itself in its full glory: The German-Dutch fraction is all for the game but the Englishman is "not dying to see it". In a desperate act of last resort, they turn to recruiting one of us from the East, but our budget is too slim and the "European Union Plane" is flying nowhere. We need to stay on the ground. Helicopter tours are also available from Warmun Roadhouse in Turkey Creek—one stop after this one—but it's like going from rain under the gutter. It's even more expensive because the chopper's rotors need more special care than the plane's wings. Purnululu is otherwise hard to access, with a conventional hatchback at any rate.

A charming shop assistant in the local souvenir shop and information centre in one is sorry for us and asks where we come from.

"Gee, I would take you there with my car if I had a four-wheel." The approximately fifty-kilometre long stretch to the Bungles is a rough ride, and we would be trying to bite off more than we can chew.

"Here you are," and to each one of us he hands out a photobook of the Bungle Bungles with super thick expensively coloured pages. "Complimentary, really," he says with a grin. "Really".

We're looking at one another. "Thank you."

"At least you're going to have nice pictures," he adds.

"That's very kind of you," we say, a bit embarrassed.

"Help yourselves to the pins or other souvenirs, anything for free, really."

We exchange even more baffled looks.

"Well, you're incredibly nice. But we really want you to keep your job."

Small section of the China Wall[14] near Halls Creek, WA

Halls Creek has an interesting natural phenomenon called China Wall—a long rock formation similar to a fence that goes for kilometres and disappears somewhere in the harsh, hilly and barren outback. The road seems like going through a private land, because after a few kilometres of gravel road there is a gate with a sign: *Shut this gate. Thanks.*

Not far from here, only some 150 kilometres or so, is the infamous Wolfe Creek Crater used for some TV creations to further reinforce the well preserved reputation of Australia as a bloody dangerous place.

We are parting with our three co-travellers in Turkey Creek Station, never to see them again. But we'll meet Harry just in a few months' time—this time in a few hundred thousand crowd at the Jazz Festival in the Sydney Domain. Australia is small.

---

14 China Wall near Halls Creek http://goo.gl/maps/Ba7V

26
Of Crocodiles and Men: Take I

From the last actual crossroad—some 830 kilometres from here—we're arriving in Wyndham, the Kimberley's northernmost town and a place that at first glance looks like the last outpost of nowhere. The town was discovered by white settlers around 1819 and they described it in such an awful way that for the next sixty years almost nobody else arrived.

On seeing the endless stretches of dry sea shore with sparkling and glittering salt all around, uninitiated travellers might be excused thinking, nothing could be more boring. But they would be wrong. In fact there are four incredible things you can't see anywhere else.

"Big crocodile" in Wyndham, WA

Australians like it big. A large crocodile is guarding the entry to the town after the first right turn. It can't be missed. It's eighteen metres long and is made of concrete. A perfect computer-designed crocodile[15]. Even the long truck parked next is much smaller. Secondly, the Big Aboriginal family[16] sculptures are not far from here.

---
15 Big crocodile in Wyndham https://goo.gl/maps/6kdWFB9LLP82
16 Big Aboriginal family in Wyndham http://goo.gl/maps/ShMZ

Another one of the big landmarks that decorate small, less significant Australian towns, dying to be known for something. There will be many more of them coming.

Big Aboriginal family sculptures in Wyndham, WA

Third is the Five River Lookout, which—as the name suggests—a view of five rivers. If you still have enough juice in you in this scorcher, the view will take the rest of your breath away.

Number four is a crocodile farm. That's where we're going now because one of the travellers we had met before knew the owner. The farm is almost at the end of the town road.

The oldest croc in service is retired and had he been a pup, he would wag his tail on hearing Bismark. Because that's his name. As the plaque near him puts it, he is seventy but feels forty. He loves life as long as there is anything to eat. And he eats everything. The scar on his back was given to him by one of his chums. So much for Bismark. His friend Oombi, in the next cell, is doing time here. In the Aboriginal town of Oombulgurri, he ate twenty-five local dogs—one of them directly from the leash. He was just about to put local children on his menu when he was captured and transported here, to his new asylum, surrounded by a harem of five females. He enjoyed them for a year or so, then got hopelessly bored. Sex wasn't his thing anymore.

We are slowly starting to understand what kind of habitat this northern Australia is surrounded by. Crocs are common in all rivers here and can swim hundreds of kilometres inland, especially during floods.

The crocodile is not an overly intelligent being. As a reptile—it's reminiscent of the ostrich in the bird world but unlike birds, he doesn't have selective thinking, which means he can't tell a white swan from a shiny red Adidas t-shirt. And so even humans can easily become part of the food chain and alas, this time not quite on top. A bird will selectively pick grains from hundreds of stones without even touching them once. A croc needs to have a bite first to see if it's worth his while.

Barren, dry landscape and dark red rocky shades escort us when we leave the town and head back south.

El Questro, sounding like a dust-covered town from one of Clint Eastwood's Western blockbusters, is disappointingly only a luxury paradise for affluently retired. It's on the Gibb River Road, the unsealed shortcut through the Kimberly from which we conveniently chickened out and blamed it on the impotence of our car. We're on its other end now and look for recompensation. But because we're not into El Questro at all. Emma Gorge, only a few kilometres before it, will more than do. It's only twenty-five kilometres from where we are now. I know, it doesn't sound much but on this gravel road it feels like a hundred. Emma Gorge has a wonderful natural pool and is luxury itself. Free. The waterfall there is irresistible. A wonderful refreshing place. It will be a perfect shower.

Tonight we'll be sleeping on a remote paddock about a hundred metres from the main dirt road. The field is rough and covered by hard rocky soil. We're pitching near a huge boab tree, far enough from the nearby water stream. The crocodile thoughts are not leaving us at ease.

Australia has a paradox. Despite all these vast swathes of land, there is often nowhere to put the tent up. The ground is so hard the hammer bends the metal pins. It's a bit like in cities where there's often an excess of space but nowhere to park cars. I wonder if the modern city planners borrowed inspiration from the local landscape.

The field is completely empty, except for occasional trees and dry shrubs. Every now and then a passing car raises dust clouds on the barely visible main road. The dust patiently settles back on its uneven surface each time. In the dark, the lights of an oncoming car are discernible for kilometres away.

Clouds of dust after a passing car

We know that because there are only a few cars driving that night. Bellows of free-roaming cows in the distance add some uneasiness to our pondering about what to do in such a place in case of a fire. Not an ideal place to spend a night, but what can we do? Kununurra is at least seventy kilometres away and we really need to have a good rest before heading there. For a good reason.

27
Castration as a Job: Kununurra

Kununurra grows each season by a good few thousand travelling workers on local farms, a large percentage of them backpack-

27 Castration as a Job: Kununurra

ers. They make the local campgrounds their temporary homes. Agricultural business worth millions of dollars thrives here because of a gigantic dam that irrigates it all. They grow everything here that the tropics can offer and then sell it all over the country.

The plan is simple: find a job for a week just to keep the momentum going. No dramas. If nothing else, we'll have some extra cash for petrol. Normally you don't get to those places unless you work there, which should be another bonus. And so we sign up to a local job agency. There are a few in the town. At the moment they have a choice of watermelon picking and something calling itself *corn detasseling*.

"It's a fantastic job! Easy, easy! You're just walking all day and—and tearing down corn tops," says a young employee of the agency in some regional British accent. She points to a sample cluster hanging on the notice board.

When filling the forms out, she is polishing her nails while giggling with somebody on the phone.

It's humming with life in the camp. It feels like a community of travellers. Mainly young guys pretty much from everywhere, and all in rather shabby-looking cars, criss-crossing Australia in all directions. An Australian guy at a watermelon plantation bursts into laughter after being told what the rates are. "It was higher five years ago!" he says. "I was here then!"

We're going to work tomorrow and can't sleep. It doesn't make sense because we're tired. What's more, the couple in the neighbouring tent was already at it shortly after lunch and are at it again. Wild passionate sex with tent canvas the only barrier between us. The left tent. Now the pair from the right tent are doing the same, only louder. It starts slowly, with tender whispers, within minutes intensifying into groans, soon culminating in slaps and spanks with some dirty talk moans between rounds. That scenario will repeat itself five times in a row. Night after night. It's like one of those TV shows, you know how they will unravel, but you're lazy to grasp for the remote so you wait out the happy ending. We badly need to sleep. We're going to detassel corn tomorrow and don't in the slightest have an idea what that means. "You're going to tear down the corn tops. Easy. Very easy."

The next morning we're trudging to the agreed spot where a minibus is to take us into the field. The guy in the khaki sleeveless shirt and green cap is about fifty and the skin on his bare arms is burnt to a cinder. He is Roger, our boss. He signs everybody in and asks if we have water. Plenty of water. Five litres each—not negotiable. So early in the morning and it's incredibly hot. Like thirty-five degrees Celsius. The car turns to a dirty unpaved road after about thirty kilometres. The 4WD van doesn't have a problem with that. The driver doesn't even bother to slow down a tiny bit. A fine thin dust slowly rising from the chassis has filled the whole interior and starts to grind between teeth. We see endless fields[17] of corn. Some have rows of baby corn, not even a metre high, with sprouts in clusters; others have ripe corn, twice as high and almost ready to be taken down.

Endless cornfields of Kununurra, WA: young corn

I was used to going through corn fields when I was a boy, but never realised how much work was going into growing it. The sort cultivated here is for people's menus and the process is even fussier. In young corn, the faulty ones are those that have grown <u>*significantly*</u> higher than the average. They should be mercilessly

[17] Giant crop fields of Kununurra, WA http://goo.gl/maps/0RLT

eradicated, by tearing them out with the roots. In more mature corn, which might be two metres and higher, only the tops are pulled out. If that sounds too easy, there are three rows of male corn plants intercut with two rows of female corn, or something to that effect.

"Owright guys," commands Roger the foreman. "We've got irrigated rows here. They were done overnight. I recommend you take off your shoes." With that, he assigns two rows to each of us and off we go.

Feet get buried deep down in the mud. Those who left their shoes on have to pull them out of the wet brown soil by hand only after a few steps.

First, we try to understand what it is that's being asked from us—which plants are good enough to be left alone and which ones deserve attention. It's not an exact science. In fact, it's very subjective. Everybody seems to be taking them down at his or her own will, being the judge and the executioner at the same time.

The twelve-member or so team is international, a jolly bunch of young people: a chatty Irish girl on good terms with the boss, a local Australian, a couple of Scots, Canadians and a Frenchmen who is all "*bien sûr et très bien, mais les langues étrangères ne sont pas son point fort*". The midday break is half an hour, it's a ten-hour shift. The drink bottles stay in the van and are reachable only after finishing the rows—sometimes kilometres away. Toilets are everywhere around. Just squat and sort it out. A helicopter sometimes flies over our heads, occasionally freezing in mid-air to blow and spread the seeds out of the males to females, in the act of hybrid matchmaking and procreation in the plant world—courtesy of modern technology.

Endless cornfields of Kununurra, WA: riper corn

Detasseling is a euphemism. It slowly becomes clear that we were quite unknowingly turned into paid sadists who mercilessly castrate the male population of corn plants by pulling off their willies—or tassels—so they can spread their semen to the other variety in next rows. The more promiscuous they are, the better offspring they will produce. The eunuchs can no longer bother females in their own rows and everybody, Roger above all, is happy.

Machines can be heard in the distance. They zipped through our rows shortly before us with high speed but poor precision, and that's where our manual labour comes in. Roger disappears from sight but frequently re-emerges out of nowhere, saying, "Good, good. You people better do it slowly and well." Okay, no problem.

At six in the evening, we're driven back to our makeshift homes. We're covered in pollen all over our sweaty bodies, stung by mosquitoes, and with tiny scrapes on hands from palms to neck. We're greeted by guys who were picking watermelons all day.

"Corn? Fucking piece of cake, mate! Watermelons—you bend all day, pick and handle heavy loads, and there are spiders, mice and other uglies everywhere."

Great, what a relief I'm thinking, scratching my itchy crotch.

The pollen is very fine and gets everywhere. Some people don't mind it at all, others might have an extreme reaction. After the first day of work, the itch takes the sleep away, and so does the loud sex in the neighbouring tent.

On the fourth day, the work doesn't go as fast. Roger is accompanied by his superior, who looks like a big wig from the company who normally manages everything from his desk somewhere, and makes everybody around him look small and insignificant. Including Roger. He walks everywhere with him and makes wild gestures. In today's rows, defects are on almost every plant. The machinist before us must have been drunk or something and so there are plenty of fixes. Doing as having been told a few days ago—slowly but well—to me, it's business as usual. The only person I see is Bien Sûr, who I use as a benchmark; a walking evidence that I am not the slowest one, although all the others have all but disappeared. He's got headphones in his ears to take the pain out of the work, and overall looks very cool and relaxed.

But only a moment later Roger materialises out of our nowhere, saying, "You guys buggered or what? You'd better not come tomorrow, mate," after which he quickly disappears again, but not before walking to the next row where he delivers the same blessed message to my French neighbour.

Bien Sûr is completely at ease, consumed by his phone, and categorically not letting anyone disturb his inner world of harmony and peace. The next morning he comes to work like normally, only to be told officially in front of everybody, "YOU'RE FIRED!"

28
Sea in the Desert: Lake Argyle

From Kununurra, it's only a stone's throw to a remarkable and one of the largest man-made water reservoirs in Australia, Lake Argyle[18]—one that in terms of its size and capacity would fit Sydney Harbour an unbelievable twenty-six times.

18 Lake Argyle, WA https://goo.gl/maps/oRHpBy349pK2

Lake Argyle dam,[19] WA

It was finished in 1972, and what used to be hilltops are now seventy or so islands. It's surrounded by a magnificently picturesque terrain and the colours at sunset on a local boat cruise are nothing short of splendid. The small boat goes to the all attractions one by one, and the guide is confident we're going to see them all. First, the rock-wallabies slowly moving around the reddish cliffs, then fresh-water crocodiles lying motionless at the shore, before jumping to water in a splinter of a second when the short proximity of the boat becomes uncomfortable to them, and then golden orb spiders who make their webs in the dry treetops. Their spider webs are so strong they can even catch small birds. NASA is said to have used them for their exceptional properties in the space suits research program, until the suits suspiciously started to remind of cocoons. But there are also spitting fish. Just drop a few breadcrumbs in the water and they will hurl small streams of water back at you. They think you are insects and want to eat you. Those weren't in any research program.

---

19 Lake Argyle, WA dam https://goo.gl/maps/J494ziv35bJ2

Golden orb spiders in dry treetops

At sunset, it's time to open wines and beers and go for a swim in the lake. The number of crocodiles here is around twenty-five thousand but hey, don't worry! "The freshie is a goodie, mate. Grab a pool noodle and have a go!" The fresh-water crocodile is said to be "harmless unless you start to mess with it. Then you can end up armless," continues a jolly woman guide in her forties. What a relief. The water is beautiful and warm. It's evening but it's not cold at all. "Or another comparison: play with a fresh-water crocodile and all you need is microsurgery. Play with a saltie and all you need is a wooden box." Well, all in all, that's enough. We don't want to catch cold, do we?

Tom and Ellyssa are a couple who travel. Later, they tell us that he used to work for a large high-tech company for fifteen years until it was swallowed up by a bigger high-tech company, and that in turn was devoured by an even larger high-tech predator. He was one of the gnawed away bones falling off the fresh corporate carcass. He didn't mind much in the end because he got a nice redundancy package and was sick of them all anyway. They bought a caravan and set out for some serious travels. She works from home and they have no children. Their caravan looks better than most luxurious city flats.

III. Broome to Darwin

Fresh-water crocodile

"Backpackers, eh?" says a giant bearded guy standing next to us selling beer at a small stall counter. When he's not doing that, he works as a local ranger—a nice chap with grumpy humour, not exactly talkative, but after two beers his tongue is coming loose. It turns out he's not just a ranger. He is a part of a water protection program, as he puts, "an anti-terrorist thing".

"When you take into account how big this lake is, somebody not in his right senses might one day want to hurt it." There was a moment of silence. He didn't say it exactly but I think what he meant by that was poison the lake.

Now some people really are weird, but how much of a fruitcake would you have to be in a forty-two degree scorcher to want to wander to the middle of a lake that is hundred kilometres long and eighty kilometres wide, in totally inaccessible wasteland, carrying—how much of the lethal stuff would be needed?—and then stagger back away to his terrorist base somewhere in Asia, solo-crossing the Kimberleys on the way as the first man in history, because surely, he wouldn't be able to get to the nearest city. They would already be after him. They know quite a lot about you the moment you enter the country now.

This guy has just been back from his OH&S meeting: Occupational Health and Safety. Those meetings are compulsory everywhere now, and they take millenniums and one of the hardest things at workplaces today is not to fall asleep before they end.

He's squinting at us and measuring from head to toe, making us feel like pests for a while, now he has been given authority to remove anybody who threatens the lake.

Lake Argyle at night

"I am telling you, go this way, that's fine," and he stretches his right hand. "But don't go this way," and he stretches his left arm. After a moment of teasing him and joking about why on earth terrorists would choose this remote barren place, he suddenly goes solemn-faced and shouts, "Two of my friends died in Bali and I will see we'll have none of that here!"

"Gee," whispers the other Australian at the table. "What has got into him?" And he quickly changes subject to fishing.

The government only rents this campground for short periods of time; usually one year, after which it has to be renewed. It's basic and worn-down and nobody seems to be keen much on attracting crowds in here. And thanks to that, this place is still pristine. A pool with beautifully warm water has three people around it.

"Now, do you want to see A FISH? We have silver cobblers here." Standing to his feet, he opens a huge outdoor freezer and a large five-kilo rock-solid frozen fish is out sitting on the table top. Its wide-open sparkling eyes are staring at us as if they wanted to tell us a story. If not for a bit of frost lying on its head, I swear I would think it's alive. The silver cobbler is a star. It used to have a boring name, shovel-nosed catfish, but the food marketers changed it and it worked. It's one of the best eating fish species in Australia.

Australia has its mystery spots. While you can still get to some of them with a bit of determination, there are some only meant for a handful of chosen ones. Parts of Lake Argyle might be in that category. In spite of its remoteness, it's a strategic place. And it's not just water. Diamonds were discovered in its southern part in Matsu Range in around 1970. With a single mine, Australia suddenly found itself in the prestigious club of top diamond producers, making one third of the world's production. Some of the diamonds are of pinkish colour and outstanding quality. It goes without saying that they don't want you and me sniffing around. And it's not exactly a place with public transport either, so even getting to the first gate might pose a problem of its own. It can be found on the Google map but only in satellite view[20]. Apparently it spans across Aboriginal sacred site called Barramundi Gap. It is now a domain of Rio Tinto, a large mining multi-national.

Other parts of the lake are known for the discovery of an interesting stone called zebra rock. It's not a gemstone but it's not found anywhere else in the world and, as the name suggests, it looks exactly like zebra skin. It was forming by layers of sediment for about six hundred million years. Quite impressive when you think dinosaurs left "only" about sixty-five million years ago.

We're meeting our ranger friend the next morning on the dam road shortly before leaving. He slows down, opens his window and mumbles, "So, you're leaving eh?" After getting some nods from us, he goes on, "Good on ya, bloody backpackers."

---

20 Argyle Diamond Mine https://goo.gl/maps/fQMpiNEjdcn

29
Customs and Public Holidays: Northern Territory Border

It's about an hour's drive from Lake Argyle to the border with Northern Territory. It's a bit like leaving a richer country for a poorer one, predominantly for one reason. When crossing to Northern Territory, you don't have to stop, but when going in the opposite direction, the Western Australians will turn your car upside down. They're not so much after drugs and weapons—not sure what they think about those—because they're only after your fruits and veggies. *Fruitcake police.* Your car must be free of anything that might in the slightest probability host the fruit flies, because if somebody smuggled them over the border they could render Roger and his boss badly unemployed. Therefore there are big penalties and the agricultural business boasts of their fly-free zone status. It can even be marked on some maps. If one single bastard fly is found, the area would lose its fly-free status and new certification and paper process would make businesses dig deep into their pockets. So, the Western Australians got it sorted out and everybody is happy. Or? Well, "We Northern Territory farmers would like those checks too." Bad luck. They are few and far between and their lobby is weak.

The one-way border moves your clock forward by one and a half hours. Another interesting oddity. However strange, it's nothing unusual because hardly anybody lives here. It's more interesting in Coolangatta in Queensland, a town bordering with New South Wales, where the popular Gold Coast airport is. From October to April, half of the town is on a different time zone due to the daylight saving time. On one side of the street it's 10 am, on the other side it's 11. Not all Australian states use daylight saving time changes.

The next twenty-four-hour rest place looks great, like always. There is smoke from fireplaces, which feels strange because it's very dry tonight.

III. Broome to Darwin

A thirty-odd-year-old caravan stands nearby. The owner's name is Ken, and it's not long before he sits at our fireplace. He used to drive with his wife; now, unfortunately, he's driving alone. He is from the older generation of gentlemen who are always nice to talk to. He brought us his potatoes because the next day they would be confiscated. He's going to WA. And so we're putting the spuds in the fire to bake and talk about times gone by.

His father was injured four times: once in Gallipoli, where the British so graciously sent their Australian and New Zealand cousins to the first line. Instead of feeling a grudge, they made it into one of the base stones of the new national identity—a legend that on April 25 each year is celebrated as ANZAC Day, with one day of public holiday as a bonus.

In 1914, when Australia was only thirteen years old, the old chums from Britain came here and said, "Howdy! There is a war out there, and we would appreciate your help in blowing up Germans. You don't have to, of course, but if *you* get busy one day, you might not have an ally. Just look north. Fifty times as many enemies are waiting at the gates. Good luck. God bless."

A desperate soldier in a Canberra museum

A strange campaign started. Poor families of new settlers were visited by army recruiters promising adventures to their sons.

Young boys in scruffy shorts were listening to a nicely dressed army officials' stories of the big world. "Do you want to travel around the globe, lad? Join us! We'll train you, son. You'll see big things. You'll help your country, your dad. You'll become a hero." The youngsters, looking at the bleak outlook of their immediate future, often said yes. The officials didn't mind that many of them were only sixteen or seventeen. They recruited about fifty thousand in Australia and about eighteen thousand of them in New Zealand. Many were sent to Asia Minor to pacify Turks, and in a selfless act of patriotism, to seize Istanbul. During landing, however, things went awry. For some reason Turks didn't like the idea and massacred them with machine-guns. With big losses on both sides, they called it off after eight months of pointless fighting.

Countries like to be built on memorials. The last ANZAC hero passed away in 2002. His name was Alec Campbell and he was one hundred and three years old.

30
Spa Time: Katherine is Hot, Douglas is Cool

People we know in Katherine live about twenty kilometres outside the town. They grow mangos and mahogany trees. The latter takes a long time but makes for a fine export item. It's used for furniture and acoustic guitars. A small forest is on the hill because floods are here almost every year.

The narrow road to their house is full of kangaroos. They don't even bother to move away. John and Jane have two hounds. They use them to chase them and occasionally finish them off in the street, practically in front of their neighbours' children. Something like a hobby. When asking them if it's not cruel to kill a cute plush animal like a roo, they only shake their heads in disbelief, "This bloody pest, you mean?"

Their house is a typical tropical dwelling with large windows and large bushy unkempt garden. A huge green frog is sitting on the porch. Both of them live off the farm but she makes extra money by teaching math and he makes social programs for the local Aboriginal community. Children have flown out of the nest and study somewhere in a remote city. Both are very well educated.

"Katherine Gorge is a beautiful place. You should go there. And don't miss the *hot springs* in the town," they say.

Knowing locals is always worth gold. They point you to places you normally don't find. Like Scout Hall. "Go off the Victoria Highway to Rundle Street and then to Campbell Terrace till you reach the end at Riverbank Drive." It is not hot but pleasantly warm. It's a natural pool with thirty-four degrees Celsius crystal clear water. It's not thermal, it's not volcanic, it is simply warmed by the earth and gushes out to the top. Pure ingenuity of nature. One could bathe all day in it. An ideal place after a long journey. In the wet season, the water level can rise by fifteen metres, then it's all under water.

While sitting in this little waterhole, there is a family with two pre-adolescent sons. For two years now, they've been touring Australia in a caravan, setting up equipment for karaoke shows in pubs. Karaoke is quite popular in the country and Australians treat their artistic performances rather seriously. Performers are rewarded with hefty applause, and for a while everybody can be a music star. The caravan is long and tows a small car behind it. Whenever they're free they look for gold with a metal detector in the outback. They show us samples they found. Some are fools gold, but they also have some real stuff. Children's mandatory school education is done by home schooling. They pass some exams from time to time to show they're not turning into apes and off they go again. They wouldn't change this lifestyle for anything, because, as the happy splashing father puts it, "Look at the beauty around. It's all my garden. And this here is my spa!"

Not far from here is Katherine Gorge, part of the Nitmiluk National Park where many interesting tracks start along the river; for instance the fourteen-kilometre long Butterfly Gorge.

30 Spa Time: Katherine is Hot, Douglas is Cool

Cascading waterfalls at Edith Falls, going for miles and miles through perfect solitude

Into the third kilometre and still not a soul around. The river goes on but the track gradually ends and we would need a canoe. We're following along the rocky walls as far as we can, sometimes crossing water and having a good swim. Water here is so nice. A snake is going up a tree and another one is resting on a big rock in front. Colourful butterflies are all around.

"By the way, last week two large crocs were spotted. They got one of them, but the other is still at large somewhere in the gorge," says our host at the dinner, serving food, showing a cheeky smile. And he takes out the local paper to prove it.

"That's okay guys. The probability is so small that we didn't want to be spoil sports. You wouldn't swim otherwise".

Edith Falls[21] are on the way to Darwin, where we're aiming for the next day, and a track there takes us up the river on cascading waterfalls to Sweetwater Pools and Upper Pools, where it feels like total isolation. The few people we meet are overseas tourists. Nobody seems to like going too far from the car park.

---

21 Cascading waterfalls Edith Falls, NT https://goo.gl/maps/43KBR8CZjJF2

III. Broome to Darwin

A local newspaper informing about crocodiles

Then it's the Stuart Highway again to take us north. It was named after a guy who, as first European, crossed the continent from Adelaide to Van Diemen's Land. John McDuall Stuart did it in 1862 and—as was not always obvious then—he also returned.

A left turn shortly after Hayes Creek goes to Daly River and Douglas Hot Springs, also known as Tjuwaliyn[22]. The last seven kilometres is dirt road and we're stopped by another big water patch. Just as we're turning around, another old 2WD Toyota is coming in our direction. A young ranger says he crossed the pool every day. No problems. The puddle doesn't look so bad, we are only worried about any big rocks that might be hiding in the murky water. We like our little hatch now and don't want it to get hurt.

---

[22] Tjuwaliyn (Douglas) Hot Springs, NT https://goo.gl/maps/XEpxD3gy12J2

Bumpy road to Douglas Hot Springs

Douglas Hot Springs can be hot all right. The name is not kidding. But it's different than the one in Katherine. It's a small creek with hot water seeping from somewhere that mixes with otherwise much colder water around it. It can be really hot at some spots and rather cold in others. You have to move and find the ideal place. If you stop moving, small fish will find you and gently touch to see if you're good to eat.

There are small towns further up north like Pine Creek—nice for a stop and refreshment. Batchelor, about thirty kilometres past Adelaide River, has an interesting landmark. A true miniature of Karlstein castle[23] stands at the corner of Rum Jungle Road and Tarkarri Road. The place is called Havlik Park and is named after an immigrant and adventurer who built it in 1978.

Cathedral Termite Mound is the next stop—a five-metre high pile of earth has been home to the plant-eating termites for over sixty years now.

Litchfield National Park might be taken for Kakadu's much smaller brother. Everything is close here and we don't have to drive far to see it all. Buley Rock Hole, for instance. First, a cormorant is showing his diving and fishing skills in the waterfall. He is so fast

23 Havlik Park with Karlstein castle https://goo.gl/maps/9Nr6Nt5gZAA2

we almost lose him from sight. Florence Falls nearby is a waterfall hole with large boulders good enough to climb and dive in the water. The water is beautifully clean. Payments for the local bush-camp are self-serviced. Just put money in an envelope and throw it in a box by the information board. There are swarms of mosquitoes in the evening. They even get through the tent netting. What's even more nagging, a bunch of loud yahoos camp next to us and they drink and yell until the hours get small. Just like sailors recognise land by squeaking sea gulls, land travellers recognise nearing cities by the number of wailing piss artists in camps. It simply has to be anticipated. But as the saying goes, God's mills grind slowly but fine; the group is repaid in the morning. They are all sore and itching. They fell asleep by the fire and the mozzies took care of the rest.

Welcoming smoke to Darwin

Fires can be spotted on the road to Darwin—the Northern Territory's capital and the only denser population hub far far around. Sometimes even large tree trunks are in flames but that's all controlled. The landscape is dry and a large pillar of smoke is billowing over the city in the distance.

31
Darwin in a Nutshell

There is a fire close to the town but nobody seems to care. Back-burning routine. Fire is a part of the landscape. Darwin[24], named after the biologist, is the most populated town of the Territory and is surprisingly upbeat and modern. Since Cyclone Tracy, who in 1974 almost flattened the city like the Japanese during WWII, it's been rebuilt and upgraded. It's making a new but sleepy impression. Streets are wide, the centre looking out into a large bay is nice and clean. It's one of those places where people come to temporarily—two, three years and then they want something new again.

A music festival is in the town right now and it's buzzing with artists and performers everywhere, small groups of alternative music from all around the world. We're watching them sing and dance while we lie on the park lawn. Hippie, relaxed vibe under open sky, colourful dresses, beads, flowers, freedom, happiness, exotic food scent and perfect climate. Mindil Beach Sunset Market seems to have all this kind of alternative lifestyle can offer. The music goes on till the late evening. The name got it right. Sunset here is amazing. A fire can be seen far in the distance on the other side of the bay. The crowded Shady Glen Caravan Park feels like a hotel after all those modest nights.

The next morning starts with somewhat burned porridge and then shopping for supplies. The afternoon is reserved for the local nude beach. Going *au naturel* in the sea a few hundred metres with water still barely up to your knees is a weird feeling so we sit for some time and look around. They say a croc was spotted a few times here before. The water is warm, the sea incredibly beautiful. There are white cone-shaped shells everywhere, and it's time to get a move on.

After the second night spent in the Hidden Valley, much cleaner and less cramped than the last camping place, we have a morn-

---

24 Darwin, NT https://goo.gl/maps/wKp3S7F9nHw

ing swim in the pool and then head south again. But before that, let's explore Kakadu, the largest national park in Australia. It's two-thirds the size of Belgium.

After twenty-nine days on the road, we've done six and a half thousand kilometres and there are about nine thousand more to get to Sydney.

IV. Darwin to Alice Springs

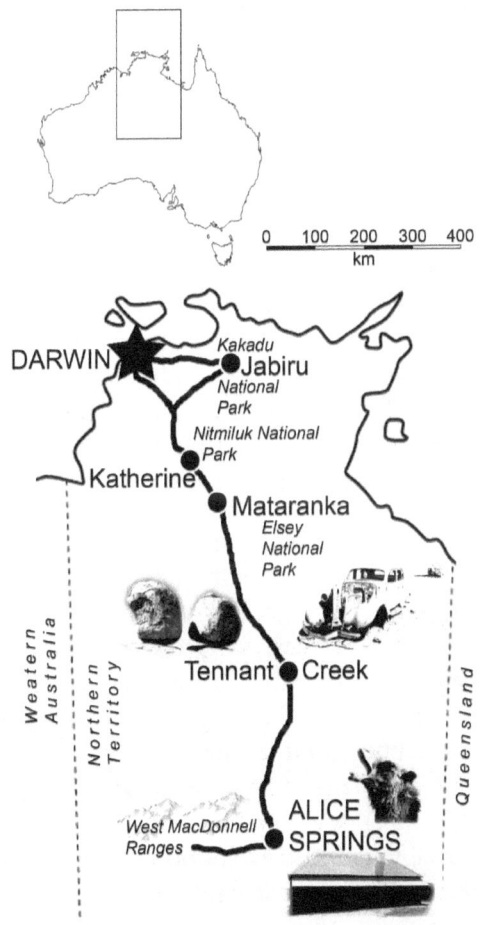

32
Where You Only Swim in a Pool: Kakadu

Sitting on a boat behind a thick acrylic glass panel, we observe a piece of hanging meat. It's going above a water surface that is unusually calm, with only a few innocent ripples. Then, as if in a nanosecond, that calmness takes the shape of a four-metre reptile beast and the meatloaf disappears under water with a loud snatch. It's fast and it comes from nowhere. A crocodile farm on the way to the park has this as a paid tourist attraction.

There is only one bitumen road going through the whole area that is as big as a small country. All other roads are 4x4 dirt roads.

"Mate, the only place you can swim here is a swimming pool in Jabiru," says a chatty Aboriginal guide in the Bowali Visitor Centre. The realisation of what a formidable creature a crocodile can be has been coming to us gradually since first entering the northern parts of Western Australia. Here you can buy a tooth as a souvenir. It's basically a miniature of a dagger. There are about seventy of them in a row; like a saw that crushes its prey with a pressure comparable only to that of a hydraulic press. Apparently, the jaw's grip is forty times stronger than the human's.

It isn't long before I ask why Kakadu isn't dubbed Moskidu. The omnipresent mosquitoes don't work night shifts but they are 24/7, like street lights. They will get everywhere—be it a tent or a car. Unlike their European *rellies*, or relatives, who normally wait till dusk, then gently and secretly enter your blood bank, steal a bit of jewelry, wipe out tracks and disappear, this kind unscrupulously perpetrates open burglary in daylight, doesn't care about noise or being shot, and completely empties your safe, after devastating the whole bloody unit. Only entomologists know why it is so, but I bet this blood-guzzling quirk of evolution is the equivalent of a croc in the insect world. It can be five millimetres long and look like a stuck pin when it's dining off you.

When pitching a tent in the Malabanjbandju Caravan Area, we rub our hands at how clever we are, finding such a nice free camping spot even though we can't pronounce its name. What a peaceful place this park is. But after a short walk through the jungle of the East Alligator River, we start to look at things differently. A big warning board makes no mistake about it: "Danger. Crocodiles inhabit this area. Attacks cause injury or death." Succinct but clear.

It's their home after all.

Crocodile warning sign

Once in the bush to the river, mozzies loom from nowhere and attack without warning. Ten minutes and we're itchy all over, run back to the car for a repellent, and in all that commotion, I somehow lock myself out. The car key is smirking through the rear window, saying: "Now, aren't you an idiot? How do you want to get me now?"

What follows is a desperate and futile attempt to break into our own car. I have hardly any skills in that area so the only other thing I can think of is a heavy spanner borrowed from occupants of the nearby van. The small rear window is the main casualty of that incident but it's a tough little bugger. It won't go without a fight. It's unbelievably hard and shatters only after three mighty hits.

Glass fragments are everywhere and I am aware that the first useful junkyards will be in Adelaide and probably only in Melbourne. There are no spare parts available through the Red Centre of Australia. We'll be driving down the whole continent with a smashed window.

In a bit of stress and having nearly run over a dingo on the way back from the East Alligator River and Ubirr Rock, we trundle back to Malabanjbandju for the worst night of the whole trip, with zillions of mosquitoes filling the space of the provisional campsite to the very last cubic centimetre. They make air raids into face: ears, nose, eyes; you name it. We can't eat, and so try to hide in the car but they've got there already through the broken window. Finally we zip shut the tent but they're already in it, waiting in darkness. The thought of a river with crocodiles just metres away isn't making this any easier.

In Jabiru the next morning, the only pool in the area is closed. It's too early. It's time for Nourlangie Rock today—a place with Aboriginal paintings on rock walls—quite a popular place. Visitors arrive in vans but not many of them walk the full loop track that goes around the rock: Barrk Sandstone Walk. The information board says it's going to take six to eight hours. That's three and a half hours of normal walking speed. It takes us up a steep hill for an outlook of Kakadu and goes back to the valley near the Nourlangie Rock Art Site[25]. We meet people there again who admire the paintings that—no matter if authentic or restored—are a good attraction for tourists and food for thought. They are said to be one of the oldest human records of its kind in the world, dating back as far as almost thirty thousand years ago.

Aboriginal paintings at Barrk Sandstone, NT

---

[25] Nourlangie art site, NT https://goo.gl/maps/vcEiL91y1YF2

It is only about fifty kilometres from Nourlangie to Cooinda—a small settlement that will do for the night. Yellow Water with river cruises is not far from here, as well as Sandy Billabong, a place of a sad tragedy, that at first reading might be a bit hard to comprehend.

33
Of Crocodiles and Men: Take II

During a hot night in the middle of tourist season, nine young backpackers with a guide are camping near Sandy Billabong. The air is hot, humid and muggy. You can't do much on those days, and thoughts circle around where you could dip in water to cool down. And this little creek nearby reflecting the moon on its surface looks so inviting. While one of them is trying to play didgeridoo, the guide Glenn has just finished washing up and rubs the sweat drops off his forehead.

"Swim, anybody?" He got their attention but they looked at one another, rather puzzled.

What about crocs? As far as he knows there shouldn't be any around here. Often he used to see Aboriginal people swimming in this kind of waterholes. Surely somebody must have been here before them because he sees some mussels lying around. This is too far from the sea for any saltie and the freshies are shy. Still, they ask him a few more times.

The guide is experienced, it can't be his first tour and he must have done this many times before. He points his torch to water and can't see any danger. Then he jumps in the water and swims. Others take off their clothes and follow. The billabong is full of happy cheers and splashing fun. It's full moon, and if not for intrusive mosquitoes it might feel like paradise.

I have to check on the next group, gestures the guide and slowly leaves water. The party goes on. Some people start to go further and deeper down the pond. When the twenty-three-year-old Isabel screams and disappears under the surface, nobody takes this seriously. When she re-emerges, her lungs are already punctured and the crocodile starts to mercilessly pull her under water. Everybody gets it by now but cannot do anything. They run out of the water in panic and scream for help. It's an ugly and chaotic scene. More people arrive and a search party is organised that finally spots and puts the crocodile to death. When they salvage the body, they have a brush with another croc. It's not a made-up story. It's 22 October 2002.

The autopsy confirms that the first attack was not fatal. Crocodiles kill by drowning most of the times and this wasn't different. Ironically this one has a damaged jaw and wouldn't survive long.

The victim's sister and all the others suffered a shock of their lives in a tragedy that in the papers reads only as another sensational curiosity.

34
Flying in the Bush: Mataranka

Kakadu Highway gets us back to the Stuart Highway the next day —the main corridor to the south. While finishing off the remaining few mosquitoes that somehow still survived in the car, we already think about what's next. Because we have to go through Katherine again, the choice is obvious: the wonderful natural spa called Scouts Hall we've already been to. What else?

"—at least it doesn't stink and you don't get your head shat on," exchange two people who must have been frolicking in water for quite some time before we arrived.

"By who?" we ask.

"The bats," they reply.

"But where?" we ask again.

"In Mataranka," they say.

34 Flying in the Bush: Mataranka

Mataranka, Mataranka. We know our next destination.

Mataranka[26] is a place that the locals talk about with a bit of hesitation in their voice. It's nice, but no thanks. It's actually nice with no buts attached. The water springs are thirty-four degrees Celsius: in our opinion there is no stench and if there is, it's bearable. What makes this place great, however, is the occasional presence of bats.

Personally, we expected to see a few hundred of them or so, dangling from the trees and so we don't even focus on them so much. When entering the local pub in search of a place to sleep, we're pointed to Mataranka campground.

"But they're here now," the guy says, not lowering his eyes from the TV screen and chewing something.

"Yeah, that's no problem, we don't mind."

"Two and a half million of them," he adds, with his eyes still glued to the screen.

What's even better—at sunset, which will be in about three hours from now, they're all going to take off and leave for nightlife somewhere far from here.

After a coffee we stand at the gate to the Elsey National Park.

The palm forest is busy. *Pteropus*, the flying fox, also known as the fruit bat, is the largest bat species in the world. The wingspan in adults can reach as wide as almost two metres.

---

26 Mataranka and Elsey National Park https://goo.gl/maps/rVE4NQcgC1m

Bats of Mataranka taking off for night-life

Some of them hang without moving from palm leaves, others fly restlessly from limb to limb, hassle and nudge one another, and generally fight for whatever last bit of space is left because the palm bush is so heavily overparked that even a small crack on the stem is good enough to hold on to. The game is about finding some shade and having some rest.

They use their huge wings as fans to cool themselves down, and their screeches—a merge between monkeys and birds—echo far into the ether. In the middle of it all, there is a pool with crystal clear water and a temperature only slightly lower than the human body. Once you get in, you don't want to leave.

"Isn't that cool? We were in Sydney yesterday and now this," say two middle-aged gentlemen indulging in water.

We're asking them how that is even possible—to get from Sydney in here so quickly. It's still something like three and a half thousand kilometres, at least.

"We flew in. There's an airstrip over there," and he reaches out his hand from the warm water to show a field behind the trees.

"Our plane is over there," says the second showing in another direction.

Later that evening, by live music of the local pub, two Qantas ex-pilots are telling us how they fly to Darwin to sell YAK-52 light aircraft to an eight-member private club. It's been sourced somewhere in Ukraine, imported, then revamped for Australian standards and is now ready to be handed over. Mataranka is only a stop-over.

"It's the best value for money aircraft you can get your hands on," they explain further.

"The syndicate put the funds together."

"Russian planes are the best, mate," dishes up the other.

"You can patch them together in your courtyard. The Americans are fitting them with all kinds of electronic bullshit. Who is to know what's what?"

"This here? A piece of cake."

They really knew their stuff. One of them travelled a lot with business to Russia. He had to take a wife of his business partner there once, a never-been-out-of-her-suburb-type woman as he puts it, and be her guide in Moscow. When he was introducing her to the biggest attractions of the city, starting on Red Square, through St Basil's Cathedral, to the Kremlin, he also showed her the Mausoleum—the *Lenin's tomb*. She was quite amazed not knowing that John Lennon was buried in Moscow.

"I almost pissed my pants," he chuckles.

Kangaroos are walking around the tents at night and our voyeuristic channel broadcasts another episode. Loud sex can be heard from the nearby tent.

We're getting up early so as not to miss the plane's take-off. Two silhouettes standing next to an open bonnet are poking around with something inside the engine. The preparation is thorough. The plane itself looks like it has just left a production line. Mataranka airstrip[27] is full of kangaroos who graze on the dew-covered grass, not realising that in about an hour or so, they'll be chased around by a hundred kilometre an hour flying machine.

YAK-52 on the Mataranka airstrip, NT

Finally, the pilots wave goodbye and take off. It takes them a few minutes to ascend enough and turn, then fly down again and parade themselves in full roar over the heads of the cheering bystanders. Everybody is waving back. They don't see us any more and the dot on the sky becomes smaller and smaller until it disappears completely.

35
Alice in Wander Land

A long stretch of road awaits us from Mataranka south—about 580 kilometres to Mary Ann Dam. There is not much to see but it's still quite a nice drive. The road goes along the railway track sometimes; one that cuts Australia southwards and where the scenic Ghan rushes along to Adelaide. It's one hell of a long straight rail track.

---
27 Mataranka airstrip https://goo.gl/maps/ArL2myKHweA2

Daly Waters[28] offers a nice stop—a pub with hundreds of souvenirs scattered around its walls—coins, notes, bits of underwear, money from all around the world, hats, shirts with messages all hanging next to each other in a silent testimony of the number of people who have visited this place before us. Outside is a wooden "Shithouse"-tagged latrine with an old guitar hanging on it.

"Shithouse" in Daly Waters, NT

After Daly Waters, a sign indicates something called Churchill Hat—apparently a rock reminiscent of Churchill with his famous cigar. It's as good as having a break anyway, so let's check this out. There is nothing even close to looking like a cigar, let alone Churchill. In the local terminology, somebody is just taking the piss or has vivid imagination.

Elliot[29] is a place with a large Aboriginal population. The day is very hot and people linger in whatever shade they can find.

"Sucks to be doing that in this heat, mate," says one to a maintenance guy on a ladder changing a bulb at the local petrol station.

"He don't mind, he's getting paid," says the other.

Stray dogs don't want to leave us alone so we push on. Renner

---

28 Daly Waters, NT https://goo.gl/maps/qqYWxYBzkkT2
29 Elliot, NT https://goo.gl/maps/ex82H4rAz6u

Springs offers Free Coffee for Driver and it comes handy.

Three Ways, about twenty kilometres before Tennant Creek, is a place that all serious travellers know quite well. It's a crossing, as the name suggests and a decision has to be made here to go Alice Springs South or to Townsville East.

Road trains park at the roadhouse. They have three and more trailers and are about forty metres long. They are only allowed in remote areas, carry all kinds of stuff and trailers have to detach before entering larger townships.

Nothing in particular is in Mary Ann Dam except a free but cold shower. Another APC night: arms, pits and crotch. There are three other caravans so it seems safe. The soil is unbelievably hard, with patches of sharp, spiky thorns defending it and shouting, *"Bugger off! Hurt your fingers, twit! We hate tents!"* But we don't listen and put it up, like every day.

Tomorrow's distance to Alice Springs is short. Only about 530 kilometres.

Old car wrecks near Tennant Creek, NT

After a casual drop to Tennant Creek, we're getting closer to a remarkable place called Karlu Karlu,[30] better known as the Devils

30 Karlu Karlu / Devils Marbles, NT https://goo.gl/maps/8d9GMmiCrLS2

Marbles—thousands of large boulders and rock formations strewn across a relatively small patch of land. They are the remnants of a huge rock mass that fell apart millions of years ago, actively assisted by water and wind, who first made cracks in them and then let them crumble into thousands of pieces. Some of them look like they're arranged on one another, round and sculptured, as if deliberately split in half, and all of that is said to lie on a massive and intact mega-sized boulder buried deep in the ground. This is how the big monolith of Uluru is going to look in a few million years.

A little bit more south and we're in Barrow Creek, which is not so much a place to stop as a part of road where the much publicised case of Peter Falconio played out in 2001. He travelled with his girlfriend Joanne Lees from Darwin to Alice. At night, they were stopped by Bradley John Murdoch who was to kill him and kidnap her. And we only know because she managed to escape. Anyway, this was exactly the kind of inspiration that the Australian horror film-makers were waiting for.

Karlu Karlu / The Devils Marbles, NT

The landscape suddenly becomes hilly. We're at the threshold to Alice Springs—the imaginary centre of Australia—and Wintersun Caravan Park is our first refuge. Alice has about fourteen thousand inhabitants and many, many, many more flies.

Later, on the same day, we see Anzac Hill with a beautiful outlook of the town

The town has a nice mix of people and we hear about *noodling* because here somewhere starts a land of opal—hydrated silica gemstone they've been extracting from these parts for decades.

The Alice Springs Telegraph Station remembers almost all the modern history—an invention that enabled sending lightning speed electronic messages ten years after European settlement there. Larapinta Trail starts right next to it and is a daring two hundred and something kilometre long walking track going west. The dry riverbed of the Todd River is its first section.

36
Road to Nowhere: West MacDonnell Ranges

After a short stop in Alice, it's time to check the beautiful mountain range to the west. West MacDonnell Ranges have a red beauty and look distant and solitary.

There are gaps between hilltops, where running creeks can be found most of the time. They've been water sources for thousands of years, and the reason for clashes between the European cattle grazers and the natives. Because of harsh conditions, settlers arrived only a few decades later. Things were as bad there as anywhere else, but the local Arrernte people were luckier at least in one regard. Their Aboriginal customs and life were documented better than any other tribe in Australia, thanks to two people: Francis James Gillen, who worked as an operator at the telegraph station, and Sir Walter Baldwin Spencer, an anthropologist interested in the subject. They gathered a large collection of facts and pictures and published them in a book. Everywhere else in Australia, changes were too rapid for anybody to make more detailed observations of Aboriginal ways of life.

Standley Chasm is one such gap with a paid entry but Simpsons

Gap[31], about eighteen kilometres from Alice, is free. There is so much to see in Australia for free.

Chasm: a place where water chiselled mountains, NT

Driving from the Ochre Pits to Ormiston Gorge[32] takes us almost to the end of the paved road, and we stay in Ormiston Campground. Going on with a conventional car from here is not recommended.

A nice couple from South Australia say they prefer a tent to a caravan because they feel younger this way.

"When you're in South Australia, drop in. We're going to show you our farm." We jot down their address.

West MacDonnell Ranges have walking tracks like nowhere else. Pound Walk, for instance, is about an eight-kilometre-long track along a hill crest. Large boulder area towards the end of the track makes an impression of being twice as large because the rock walls mirror against the perfectly calm water surface. We have just

31 Simpsons Gap, West McDonnell Ranges https://goo.gl/maps/dbSosh9iYbr
32 Ormiston Gorge, Northern Territory https://goo.gl/maps/pGb4jWPY9QB2

walked into a highest-definition, 3D picture.

Perfect symmetry of the Pound Walk, NT

A howling dingo wakes us at night, and for the first time we notice cooler temperatures.

Mount Sonder is our next goal. We need to get to the base first, which for us might represent a bigger problem than the climb itself. We ask the ranger about the road quality, then point to our car.

"Sure, no problem. It's a good road," is the answer.

Eleven kilometres of the paved road really is okay, then a typical bumpy corrugated road, but there are another twenty-five kilometres of much harder surface following that, and the ending near the provisional car park at Redbank Gorge, at the foot of the mountain, is for the 4WD enthusiasts. No kidding. We have to leave the car about a kilometre from the destination. The road has deep recesses and in turns goes up- and downhill steeply.

The information board estimates the hike to take eight hours. It's sixteen kilometres return and it's not marked very well. After an hour's ascent it starts to dawn on us how small and insignificant we are in the vast, wide-open terrain. We almost lose sight of each other among thousands of rocks. A person only a hundred metres away perfectly merges with the surroundings and can no longer be seen. Now tell me something about efficiency of plane rescues. Let's stick together. The next five kilometres is a crest walk to the summit.

And those flies, flies, and flies; all around, the most annoying kind to exist on the surface of this planet. When one of them lands on your eyelash, your hand instinctively moves to get it off, but for them this is an invitation; there are ten new sitting on it now and the one on the eyelash is still sedulously licking. Their queue is very very long. This is really the time to wear fly nets on the head. It's pain in the neck but the lesser evil.

Mount Sonder / Rwetyepme, NT: 1,380 m ASL

The summit is worth the effort. The scenery around is unlike anything else. Standing in the middle of it, all we see is a landscape carved by nature for millions of years. The terrain misses any logic or pattern: it's total chaos of shape and breathtaking harmony at the same time. Hundreds of kilometres of nothing, where people are as rare as hen's teeth.

Mount Sonder is the last section of the Larapinta Trail that started at the telegraph station in Alice. For a moment, we feel like we did it all.

IV. Darwin to Alice Springs

A good hiker needs five and a half hours instead of the proposed eight for this track but it's already getting dark when we start driving back. If we have bad luck and get a flat tyre now, we're staying here for the night. A torch was left in the tent. A basic mistake. The darkness here is pitch-black. We wouldn't see a thing.

*

We have to replace a slowly leaking tyre in Alice, and replenish supplies. The Ghan Museum[33] is not far away, with a few fine steam locomotives on display. The Old Ghan was going through towns where there is no paved road today and where only a handful of people now live permanently. Ghan is a short for Afghan, to remember the Afghans who facilitated the first camel trains for expeditions linking the north with the south of Australia through the Red Centre. The British Empire had its resources everywhere around the globe then and that's when the telegraph came in handy.

"Kabul? Stop. Pls send camels. Stop. Horses turn to popcorn. Stop."

Not far from Alice on a camel farm, we're trying to visualise how hard this exercise must have been. After only a few-minutes ride, the butt starts to be pretty sore. Poor rider comfort, however, is the price for an incredibly economic performance. It's the only "machine" that runs on water. Amazingly, it gulps 120 litres of it on the spot, burps, and then walks for a week, with heavy burdens loaded all around its back, without a single thought about being thirsty.

---

33 Old Ghan Museum near Alice Springs, NT https://goo.gl/maps/rpXEh-MagDfF2

Old Ghan not far from Alice Springs

We swap the camel back for our hatchback and head for the next right turn. After two and a half hours, we're there. We get set for the night because it's getting dark. Uluru is still around 250 kilometres away. Erldunda Caravan Park is an ideal place to prepare for one of the most enigmatic places in Australia. It's also the first time we meet Alex.

37
On a Bike Through Desert

"Where have you come from?" we ask a fit young guy, expecting a large Australian city as an answer.

"London."

"Pardon?"

"From London."

"On a bike? How long did that take?"

"About five months," replies a very modest-looking Singaporean.

IV. Darwin to Alice Springs

Alex is doing a round trip of the world on his trekking bike and he started in London. Australia from north to south is his penultimate section. The last one will be New Zealand.

He paid a speeding ticket in Romania, apparently the only country in the world where police bothered to fine cyclists for speeding because the fines were bigger than their monthly salaries. On the other hand, the only place he could not ride were parts of China where he didn't get a permit. He was bitten by dogs a few times. A stray Fido took him down from his bike once and got a good taste of his bum. He had punctured about twenty-five tyres and had constant breakdowns but he's been patiently fixing everything with the tools in his small box.

Alex is tired. We can see that. Driving is easy. You sit and watch scenery. But stop and get out. Even on a sunny day, all across the outback, on this endless plateau, you will feel a mild but steady wind that's there all the time. Its only purpose is to give you hell of a hard time if all you rely on to move forward are your muscles.

Unlike Brian who we met before with a bob trailer, Alex has only his bike and a backpack. Inside it, his small stove, gas container, kettle and other necessities to get by and survive. Going around on a bike is easier said than done, that's for sure.

A cyclist on a ride around Australia on the Stuart Highway[34]

34 What it's like to be a cyclist on Stuart Highway, NT https://goo.gl/maps/rpX-EhMagDfF2

37 On a Bike Through Desert

"I'm not turning to Uluru," says Alex. "Five hundred kilometres is too much of a detour for a bike."

"Then we'll see you again in three days."

"Three days are not enough," he says after a pause. "That's Uluru, Kings Canyon, Kata Tjuta."

"We only want to spare two nights."

"Well, good luck then."

# IV. Darwin to Alice Springs

V. Alternative Look At Red Centre

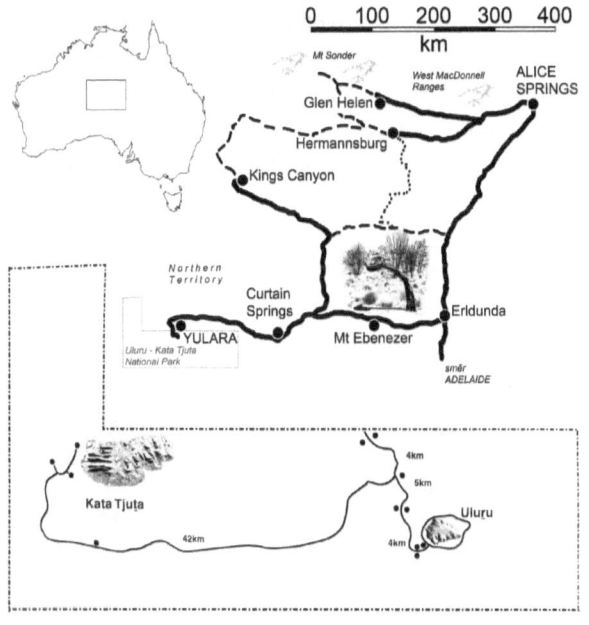

38
Where Things Howl: Uluru aka Ayers Rock

Our Swedish friends warned us. The rangers will not tolerate you sleeping rough in such popular tourist places. They will wake you up at four in the morning and waive you goodbye until you leave. Total seclusion or not, it is a national park: not allowed. Not on the road anyway. It happened to them in Kings Canyon.

We're planning to do all three—Uluru, Kata Tjuta also know as the Olgas, and Kings Canyon—for as little money as possible. It's a very touristy place and it might be quite an ambush on the wallet. Internet searches produce endless lists of resorts and restaurants and that is the last thing we're after.

We stop at Mount Ebenezer Roadhouse, where there is an art exhibition by local artists. An Aboriginal woman on a noticeboard article sheds some doubts over the authorities' push to limit climbing the sacred rock, putting it down to mainly Aboriginal disapproval. It has apparently more to do with safety and preventing injuries and fatal incidents, something that nobody, especially the local Aboriginal community, wishes to be happening.

"False Uluru": *Atilla / Mount Conner,*[35] NT

Not long after setting out from Mount Ebenezer, a silhouette of a large flat mountain is shaping up on the horizon. Atilla, also known as Mount Conner, is a "false Uluru". It's large, and quite impressive, even from the road. It is an *inselberg*, or island mountain, and it's remarkable because the top of it is what Australia used to be like many millions of years ago. The land all around it simply eroded because it knew that humans would once need roads to haul tourists in air conditioned buses, and looking at nothing would be part of the five-hour trip deal from Alice Springs.

Atilla is the last soldier standing. There is no public access to it because it's in the middle of a private cattle station called Curtin Springs. Technically speaking, it's a big rockery in somebody's giant garden.

35 Atilla/Mount Conner, NT https://goo.gl/maps/6E5sQ8azKyq

Desert art on the way to Red Centre[36]

The tourist money machine revolves around the one that comes next: a well-recognisable image icon that stands above all others. It is a place that everybody knows.

Uluṟu and Kata Tjuṯa were returned to the traditional owners as part of the native title to land policies. Their cultural heritage for Australia is so significant that the Aborigines leased the area to government for ninety-nine years back in 1985. In the 1980s, one could come here and camp at the very base. It's unthinkable today.

A half-naked local woman is dancing on the film screen of the classy cultural centre, set up in the close vicinity of the Rock. There are lots of handmade high-quality wooden souvenirs that, although nothing like the tawdry rubbish in city markets, are rather expensive. Interesting pictures and facts are shown on the walls. Some of them are covered because Aboriginal culture holds showing deceased persons' photographs, voices or even names as disrespectful. When driving around the Rock, small, slowly-moving, ant-like characters are recognisable against the blue sky horizon. They go from where the climbing track starts to the top. When it's too hot, too wet or there are otherwise unfavourable conditions, the access is closed. Bad luck.

---

36 On the way to the Red Centre, NT https://goo.gl/maps/uoWHtkQDjNx

V. Alternative Look At Red Centre

The sky is without a single cloud today. The Rock is impressive but not so much the fabricated infrastructure that surrounds it. It's two different worlds.

"Car sunset viewing area", "Car sunrise viewing area", "Bus sunset viewing area", "Bus sunrise viewing area".[37] Everything is ready.

It's afternoon and the "Car sunset viewing area" is empty, without a soul. The picture is like a postcard but tourists are still showering in the hotels of Yulara. The Rock can wait.

About twenty-seven kilometres before Yulara, there is a nameless twenty-four-hour rest place. In fact, there are a few of them on Lasseter Highway and they are small discreet veinlets going off the main road[38]. They are not marked and are hidden behind embankments and so a bit hard to find. We drive slowly. About a hundred metres behind the road, down the red sand path, there is a small area, with scattered dry trees, a makeshift fireplace, and a rusty wreck of an old 80s car with its door wide open. Otherwise, there is not a soul. The sun is still hot enough for a provisional shower from our tin can. Before we know it, it's dark. The tent is already up but it's not a good feeling. We're on our own, out of sight, off the main road, where only a handful cars drive at night.

A car engine wakes us up at 1 am. A quick peek out of the tent reveals a set of headlights coming in our direction. The stories about vanished tourist spring back to memory. Clutching a penknife in my pocket, just in case, I cautiously greet the strangers. They are two backpackers from Austria, and after throwing more wood in the fire we chat for another hour. But we have to get up very early to see the sunrise.

---

37 Uluru Sunset Viewing Area, NT https://goo.gl/maps/vSjkTxsBGdy
38 "Hidden" and free: rest areas near the Red Centre, NT https://goo.gl/maps/8x-ZjuUeismA2

38 Where Things Howl: Uluru aka Ayers Rock

A car wreck in a hidden rest area near Yulara

*

The Rock is completely different from yesterday. Today there are fast-moving clouds that drop shadows like giant magic curtains, in turns unveiling a wide spectrum of colours. This monolith has been standing here for millions of years, in sun, rain and wind, whether some now extinct animals were running at its foot or a coach of overseas tourists was taking pictures of it, no matter if baking dry in scorching sun or soaking wet in gushing streams of water after a long storm. It's almost like an artwork in a big open-air museum waiting for thieves to come and steal it. We climb poles and walk on others' heads to get that one perfect copy of the original to take home and own it, to "immortalise" the eternal for our short-lived mayfly existence. It's hilarious, and embarrassingly sad and pathetic at the same time.

Understandably, with so much beauty concentrated in one small place there is a high danger of a spontaneous artistic nuclear fusion and the government had to step in and bring it all under control. The authorities usurp the right for commercial use of the Red Centre icons imagery. Consequently, you should use no pictures of them whatsoever, either from social media, Google internet searches or any other publicly accessible source, unless you come in person, get a permit and take your own, or buy a thick, multicoloured, two-kilogram landscape photography book. Long live regulations! Who owns the Rock now?

The trail up the mountain starts at Mala Walk Parking Area[39]. A plaque commemorating those who died here is attached to the wall: mainly heart conditions and falling accidents. If the official track is followed, it's safe. Those who fall are busybodies tempting fate, going too far over the edge. The physical implications of it are quite simple. One minute I am standing firmly on my two feet, a little later the ground becomes a slope, and finally the slope becomes a wall. And because I don't have bristles or suction cups like insects to walk up walls, the gravity takes over long before I even know it. However, that won't happen on the marked track.

The first half is a steep climb along a metal chain, not a big problem for a fit person. Then it's just the walk on the top along a thick, white, dashed line that marks the highest points. Recesses made by lightning bolts are Uluru's scars. They look a bit like moon craters on some of those NASA close-ups.

On my way down, I meet panting people who crawl on the chain.

"How's it going?"

"Good. How's it going?"

"Is it far to the end?" they ask.

"Naaa, it's just this steep part, then it's all right."

"Good on you, mate," is their reply.

A guide who looks like a personal trainer is giving a boost to his student, "Come on! Don't give up! You can do it!"

She hardly catches her breath as she dangles on the chain. "No I can't, I can't."

As soon as I get down, I realise I left my hat near the top when

---

39 Mala Walk Parking Area https://goo.gl/maps/SuwqwUGA1CT2

I sat to enjoy the view. In this sun I need it. I will have to go up. Again. Quickly.

"How's it going?" the same people ask me on the way down.

"Good. How's it going," I reply.

"Is it far to the end?"

"Naaa, it's just that steep part, then it's all right."

"Wait, have we met—? A *déjà vu*—" they say, as if not sure what to say. "Good on you, mate. Good on you, mate."

It's pity we don't have a chance to speak to the true natives. They are tucked away in their communities in a permit-only territory, quite away from this place, in parts of the land that is governed by a combination of the Australian law and their customary law. It can be a perfectly orderly community or one with fifty times higher than average crime rates. The government is kind of trying to tackle this but it's not something it likes to trumpet to the world. It's still an open wound with some tousled, loose, detached bandages covering it.

Apparently, the first white man who saw both Uluru and Kata Tjuta was the English immigrant and adventurer Ernest Giles, who was exploring the area as early as in 1872. There was no naming convention on newly discovered landmarks and the best bet was to chose the name of your boss, sponsor, some kind of royalty or—if you wanted your name on it—not to return. Giles was lucky for returns, less lucky for being associated with places he had discovered. His friend Alfred Gibson was the opposite. The whole desert bears his name in memoriam. He went missing on one of Giles' expeditions.

These were real explorers, members of the toughest trade; not like us, sissies loaded with conveniences of modern life. Giles actually just saw Uluru from some distance and didn't have much time to play with names. However, he had a few ideas in store, like that of his Anglo-German patrons such as Sir Ferdinand Jacob Heinrich von Müller. One year later, his competitor William

Gosse bumped into the Rock and this time he didn't hesitate to name it after his employer, South Australian premier Sir Henry Ayers. The original name Uluru was apparently only heard around 1903, "What? *Uluru*? What a mouthful! This will never catch on!" The natives had to wait for ninety years to include it in the official name. It should read with the underlined *r*, the so called *retroflex approximant* consonant, as pronounced in the word *red* in Texan drawl. But it's very rarely used in writing.

Uluru needs to be looked at from many angles. It's different from each and every one.

39
Sexy Walls: Kata Tjuta and Kings Canyon

Kata Tjuta means "many heads" in the local lingo. There are about thirty-six of them, they say, but they are not for tramping. They are far too high anyway, so we stick to the walking tracks that lead among them. Luckily, the seven-point-five-kilometre Valley of the Winds[40] has got it all and more, including a very distinctive pattern on one of its walls that, believe it or not, officially doesn't exist. Some people recognise it instantly, predominantly guys, but many people just walk on without ever noticing. With just a little bit of imagination and a tad of American-style prudishness, we have a perfectly R-rated Ladies' Privates Rock. A beautiful piece of natural art that no official tourist guide will tell you about: Rocky Open Legs.

While Uluru is more or less a smooth monolith, Kata Tjuta has more of a wrinkled rock surface, shapes that sometimes appear to be glued together. The sun on the Walpa Gorge Walk—probably the most popular walk by most visitors because it's closest to the car park—is making those shapes unbelievably vivid, especially one hour or so before the sunset. Which means, by the way, that it's time to get out of here. Yulara is fifty kilometres away and Curtin Springs, the next free official spot to stay overnight, is eighty-six kilometres.

---

40 Kata Tjuta Valley of the Winds, NT https://goo.gl/maps/tteab6tLD8r

Yulara means "howling" in the local Aboriginal language, which most likely comes from dingoes, and possibly from tourists reacting to the exaggerated price of everything that can be bought in this small kitsch town. Just about the only thing that's cheaper here is petrol and so we're in a hurry to get some. It's getting dark, and darkness might mean trouble. With enough bad luck, a well-built kangaroo can turn our car into a worthless pile of junk, as if it wasn't close to it anyway. Just as the petrol station is around the corner, a siren wails. Police cars are different in each state and we haven't seen one until now. We are getting an ultimate farewell souvenir—now quite a common and integral part of Australian folklore—a forty kilometres per hour speeding ticket. If you don't get at least one while travelling, your luck is out of this world. You'd better start playing Powerball.

Now only one third of the puzzle is missing: Kings Canyon. From Curtin Springs the next day, we start at 9.30: we're walking on its rims early in the afternoon. The drive to Watarrka National Park was longer than expected. The canyon rocks are different again from both Uluru and Kata Tjuta—a bit like small rocky bee hives. The walls are really steep and it is a long, long way down with no railing at the top. If you slip and fall, you will find yourself in Eden, both physically and metaphorically. That's what the natural oasis at the bottom of it is called, with crystal-clear water creeks, lush greenery and trees, and lots and lots of birds. There already were a few tourists who took the shortcut from Kestrel Falls. We chose the longer way, by walking track to Lost City, then back to the top. The Kings Canyon Rim Walk is six kilometres long.

40
Coroner on Vacation

While putting the tent up back at the Mount Ebenezer Roadhouse, we notice a jolly guy sitting by fireplace. Gary is about fifty and from Melbourne. His young wife passed away some years ago. Cancer. He's been working like mad ever since, and this is his first holiday in ages. He is articulate, bright and funny. He is a coroner.

Gentle music is coming out of his huge 4x4 with tractor-like wheels. The radio has some issues because occasionally it goes scratchy, and each time, without ever going off his subject, Gary brings it back to life with a mighty punch on the caravan wall. He's taken long service leave and travels like he used to, because this way it feels as if his wife was still with him. He speaks to her when driving and she replies to him, just like that. But then he cheers up, "They owe me. I've been working for them for all those years. I need a break! You wouldn't believe what kind of cases I get. You know what happened to me recently? I have this junkie on the table, a homeless guy. I couldn't believe my eyes. His singlet was the same colour as his skin. No, no. It was part of his skin. You couldn't scrape it off. It was like, like, his own body. Those people! And that's why I love scaring my niece shitless, 'TAKE DRUGS! They will haul you on my desk and dissect you down to the finest detail, to the smallest, tiniest particle. I will have you chopped up, just remember that, you little brat, if you ever, EVER try any drugs!' Or another champ! He had a whole bottle of Coca Cola firmly shoved up his anal canal. How was it even physically possible? Un-fucking-believable!"

A few more morbid cases follow from his long forensic experiences until we talk about famous stories, finally bumping into a true classic.

"Yeah," he sighs. "The dingo. I am telling you. She bloody well did it."

41
Busting Dingo

On 17 September 1980, a two-month-old Azaria disappeared from her parents' tent, and despite an exhausting search operation of three hundred plus volunteers, the baby was never found. A week later, her bloodstained clothes and nappies were found. When police asked the parents Michael and Lindy Chamberlain what had happened to their child, the parents gave them a grim answer: it was taken by a dingo. The case was forwarded to the forensic investigator, the blood analysis seemed to reveal Azaria's blood on the back seat of their Holden, and that was the main corpus delicti. The suggestion was that the mother could have killed her with a knife. Nevertheless, there were lots of dingoes spotted around the campground that night and witnesses had heard a crying baby and believed the parents.

They started to shoot dingoes in the vicinity of the Rock in an attempt to find human remains in their stomachs. They even tried to experiment what dogs might do to a chunk of meat wrapped up in baby sleepers. A media circus began feeding millions of people every day with speculations. Tip-offs of all kinds were coming in, about the parents being religious fanatics; she was a witch because she was only dressing in black; it was done by their son who they were now covering for, and so on and so forth.

A year and a month later, almost to the day, police searched the Chamberlain's home and seized about three hundred objects, including the car, which gradually led to a murder charge. The trial was all about what little evidence the prosecution had found. There was little proof against her, but even less against the dingo. The jury finally decided she was guilty and the court sentenced the then pregnant Lindy to life in prison. She appealed this within a year but with no success. New facts were coming to light, most importantly one overturning the hypothesis about blood in the car; there were groups and campaigns lobbying for her release, but all in vain. And that seems like a plain ending to an immensely sad story, but that's only about half of it. Sheer chance took care of the rest. An English backpacker, David Brett, arrived on the sacred Rock to untangle the case once and for all.

In 1986, he decided to climb the Rock in darkness and alone. He went too close to the edge and gravity sent him crashing down hundreds of metres to the earth, falling to his death. Eight days later, when his body was finally found, around an area with a large number of dingo lairs, they chanced on a piece of clothing that turned out to be Azaria's jacket. New speculations saw that the case was finally reopened. In about two years, the parents were acquitted and released but the public opinion was still split and media still hungry. Only there was not so much to feed on any more.

In 2004, a retiree claimed that in 1980 he had shot a dingo with a dead infant in his mouth. He only wanted to testify after twenty-four years or so because he had shot the dog illegally and was afraid of the penalties. Police wrote the details down and made another record in their big database of loonies. Only in 2012, thirty-two years after the tragedy, a coroner pronounced a final ruling on Azaria's death: she was killed by a wild dingo. The sobbing mother's cry at her first interview has turned into an Australian cult phrase. "A dingo's got my baby!" says Gary. That's what's left of the famous case.

42
Where Mad Max Drove: Breakaways

Kulgera, a small settlement with a petrol station, is about a two-hour drive from Mount Ebenezer. It's noon when we cross the border to South Australia. Cadney Homestead Roadhouse is a little bit further south, and that's where we meet Alex for the second time. He's fixing his super-thin road bike tyre. Another puncture. He has a friend now, a sixty-year-old Japanese guy, Sumio, also on a trip through the centre. The weather change has made itself felt on the cyclists' faces.

Sumio is a big fan of Go, a very old Chinese board game, possibly the oldest board game in the world. There are whole online tournaments. Sumio explains. "Unlike chess, the board is bigger, the rules seem very simple, with only white and black stones, but strategically the game is very complex. It's all about gaining more territory, while playing on multiple parts of the board at the same time."

Strange landscape of Breakaways, SA[41]

We're going south in the morning. About thirty-two kilometres before Coober Pedy, a tiny left turn takes you to Breakaways, an independent mountain range that, as the name implies, broke away from the bigger Stuart Range. It wasn't yesterday, but rather around the time dinosaurs had vanished. Moreover, it was covered by sea. After eleven kilometres of a decent unpaved road, a very strange landscape opens before us. What used to be seabed many millions of years ago has turned into a unique spectacle: scenery without any regularity or rule, which is why film-makers love it so much, most notably the creators of Mad Max.

Going further would take us to the dog fence that protects pasturelands of the south from the wild dingoes in the north. It's 5,300 kilometres long.

By the way, our journey is about in the middle now: the fortieth day on the road and there are six and a half thousand more kilometres to go. That's shortly before Coober Pedy, one of the most enigmatic places in Australia. What's there can't be found anywhere else.

---

41 Strange landscape of Breakaways https://goo.gl/maps/bS4etxuyWCL2

V. Alternative Look At Red Centre

VI. White Bloke Down a Pit

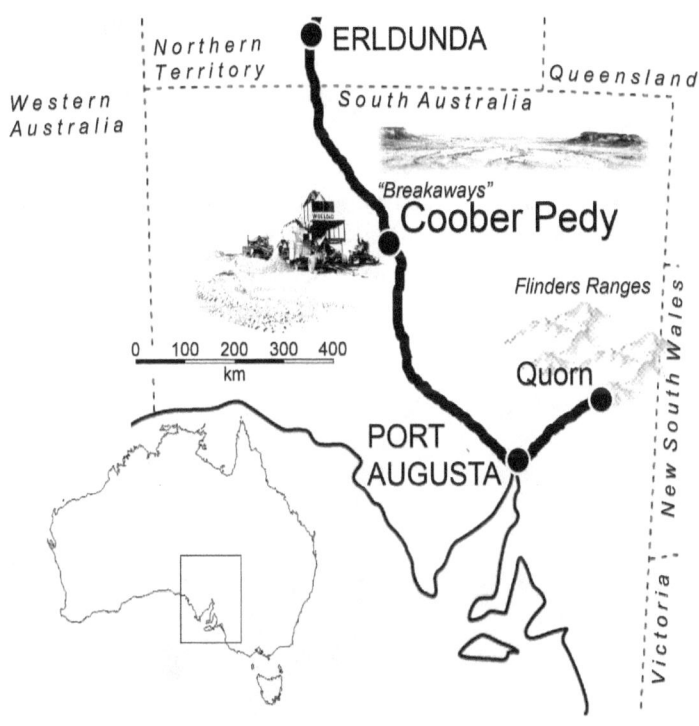

43
Opal Land: the Ingenuity of Coober Pedy

The name evokes thousands of holes, pits and shafts, dug out for miles and miles far beyond the town. Even before entering the place itself, we can't help thinking, we're in some kind of weird giant industrial zone, searched through over and over again by heavy machinery, ending as one superbig ant heap.

It's windy and cold. It's not that hot Australia that one sees on postcards. A big nicely coloured dumper truck on hoisted legs marks a symbolic entrance to the town[42], suggesting this will be a home to heavy duty. Warning signs are everywhere. "Don't run", "Don't walk backwards", "Beware, deep shafts", "Unmarked holes", "Blasting", "Penalty for unauthorised entry to mining claims"[43]. There were a good few who ended stuck with their heads down. The town itself makes quite a good dusty impression: rough but pleasant. The main paved road branches off to unpaved roads, where we dodge piles of debris that are actually houses. They call them dugouts and they can be anything from people's homes to churches—Catholic, Orthodox, Serbian, Greek, and even a dugout camping ground. All rugged, covered in dust, and very original.

Warning signs shortly before Coober Pedy, SA

And then there are the opals. That's how it all started.

The beginning of the twentieth century was not particularly kind to many immigrants. People were chasing money wherever they could, and when they didn't have any, they could simply starve. Real poverty without any cushions. In 1915, a four-member expedition set out to explore the outback on camels. They were there to look for riches of the land. Their main problem was wa-

---

42 Truck as a symbolic entrance to Coober Pedy https://goo.gl/maps/yRePYG5MbBL2

43 Warning sign before Coober Pedy https://goo.gl/maps/M2uzbhWsT4F2

43 Opal Land: the Ingenuity of Coober Pedy

ter. There wasn't enough of it anywhere and all explorers were depending on finding it, otherwise they'd have to head back. This group was no exception. The heat and drought were unbearable. The temperature was high, above forty. Looking for water took an excessive amount of time and they only had enough for a few more days. The fifteen-year old Bill Hutchinson was assigned to look after the campsite in the morning, when three older members set out to find some water. On their return, the fire was out and Bill had disappeared.

"Where the hell is he?" thought his father.

Anger was soon replaced by worry, and when it got dark the chances of finding him quickly dwindled. They put more wood in the fire and hoped he would see it and find his way back.

"Where have you been? Didn't I tell you to look after the camp!?" exclaimed his father when Bill suddenly appeared.

"Look!" says Bill.

"You could have died out there—!"

But Bill wasn't listening. He'd found water and this little strange stone called opal, which he first thought was some desert rubbish. After spreading the news in Adelaide, a new kind of fever unleashed itself. More and more people arrived to dig in the ground. Deeper and deeper.

And the natives, thinking that something's not quite right with those white men, must have shaken their heads in disbelief, saying, "Kupa piti." "Kupa piti."

The white bloke is sitting in a hole!

That's how the town is said to have got its modern name: Coober Pedy.

The business went well, until the Great Depression that almost brought it to ashes in 1931 and turned the place into a ghost town.

Everybody seems to have something to do with opals here. At a petrol station, hotel or a museum, everything shines in opal.

"Buying opal", "Opal dealer", "Opal Inn", "Opal displays", "Opal shop", "Opal gallery", "Opal cutter", opal this, opal that. As for the wholesale, the Chinese are said to be doing well selling it to their enormous market, increasingly hungry for luxury items. The local retail is very diverse.

Beautifully rough: Coober Pedy from a hotel roof and a spaceship left behind by film-makers,[44] SA

Small sandpits set up in front of many shops invite people to noodle: rake for traces of common opals, or potch, which is opal without much colour or worth.

We are in a shop owned by a German family who has been in the area for a long time. There are black and white pictures all around the walls, showing their humble beginnings, he and his wife sitting in their own dugout living room. He arrived in Australia with nothing, and from a city he came to the end of the world here to spend years by digging in the ground. He's worked his way up. At the moment he is at a trade fair somewhere in Germany, doing business selling opals.

---

44 Spaceship left behind by film-makers in Coober Pedy, SA https://goo.gl/maps/C2ujytDvn182

43 Opal Land: the Ingenuity of Coober Pedy

The nicer potch stones are sold as souvenirs for small amounts, because the more colour, the more dollars. A Croatian shop assistant has been here a long time too.

"There are people from everywhere. Any nationality," she says.

In a cosy restaurant down the street later that afternoon, we meet an exceptionally nice lady and her son. Though Brenda has been here for many years, even her son Joey still speaks a charming variant of Czech.

"I had a lot of aunties and uncles over there in Czechoslovakia, you know, but they all *fried*—" he says after some conversation.

"*Died*, you mean?" we're volunteering some help because we're culturally close.

"Oh, *died*, of course, *DIED*!" bursting into laughter. "Sorry, I am confusing the two."

Brenda comes from Moravia and used to be good at car racing. But she was not in love with the regime and so she and her Slovakian husband chose to flee. Then Joey was born as a true Czecho-Slovakian Australian who used both languages with his parents until he found English was easier. Her husband passed away a few years ago and she lives with Greg, her second partner.

Joey jokes that most of the time he swaps the words *kostel* (church) for *postel* (bed) and *zaludek* (stomach) for *zalud* (glans penis), because they are kind of similar. The truth is, he speaks without any major problems.

They have a beautifully equipped kitchen and we offer to cook something traditional they would know, like goulash stew, which is more Hungarian but it doesn't really matter. Okay, deal. We do a round trip of the town first, seeing an underground opal mine on the way, plus a few more opal shops; and with ingredients, we march back in, ready for some action. The kitchen has everything we need. There are loads of people coming and going: here is a guy as big as a mountain, in a boiler suit covered by at least a millimetre layer of dust, there are others who frequently come and go like in an open space office, there is a young blonde who whispers something in Joey's ear, gives him a gentle hug and then disappears.

"I'll be back in twenty. Just need to give somebody a ride," says Joey.

Greg is Brenda's boyfriend. He works as a relief teacher in the local public school. But he is also a part-time treasure hunter. After work, he spends hours outside town noodling.

The dinner is done but it's still early. He asks me to go to school with him to do a little job. We'll be back in twenty minutes. He greets everybody as we drive along. I figure he must have been here for a long time.

He needs to cut some planks for a new shelf and the school has a perfect workshop. In Coober Pedy, practical skills are more than crucial. "Fix your car? No problem. How much did they ask for the filter? Noooo! You must be kidding. Well, mate, they ripped you off. I would have done it for you for free in five minutes. Remember, never look like a tourist or they will eat you alive."

44
Indigenous Versus Mainstream: Take III

When Greg takes me through the town, he spots a local Aboriginal crossing the street. He wears a thick loose-fitting coat, a worn knitted hat, and a long scarf that is partly covering his face. It's cold, quite cold now. He carries a bottle in his hand and is staggering a bit on the dirty roadside. He gets Greg's attention.

"Do you know how old this guy is?" he asks.

I turn my head to have one more glimpse.

"Not sure. Sixty?"

"This one is around forty, I know him. He's only going to live a few more years," he adds after a moment. "It's sad how they live," he continues. "They only eat canned food, white bread, no vegetables. They are malnourished, they don't have enough vitamins, basic nutrients. They end up with diabetes or heart condition. And that's not counting the booze. They live seventeen years shorter in average. Those who live to fifty-five can consider themselves lucky."

Shortly before getting to the school, Greg meets his colleague, a female teacher. A short exchange and he drives on. "Nice girl, but she needs better English to be a teacher. The young ones speak too colloquially and pass the blabber to kids."

We get out of the car. The school workshop is so state-of-the-art it could as well be a small factory. There are all kinds of machines, from simple table drill presses to quite advanced lathes.

I can't help returning to the previous subject and so he clamps his wooden planks and between cutting sounds of the circular saw, I listen to what he has to say.

"The Aboriginal way of life is actually 'communism' in its purest form. Property is common to the group—they have a different concept of ownership. Any competition is regarded as undesirable. That's simply their way to survive. Once somebody is sticking out from the crowd, that's unwanted behaviour and they are reprimanded, or even excluded from the rest. It makes sense to them but it's hard for us to understand. You have to turn everything you think about possessions upside down. There was this huge clash. Non-materialistic culture and highly materialistic culture went head to head and guess who won. I was always asking myself why the Aboriginal children never wanted to make anything in practical workshops. Then I found out that anything they would make at school would automatically be confiscated at home. Parents or uncles, it doesn't matter. The elders have even more say than the parents. They can punish the kids. Let's say we make a wooden chair from those planks, the boy brings it home and they chop it up and burn it as fuel for communal warmth. Or anything else. They will grab it from him the moment they see it. So why would a child want to make something at school? And they have a different sense of time. They were never obsessed with it. It's like time doesn't exist for them. They show up at school for two days and then disappear for a week. That's the stuff that makes the whites not want to send their kids to the same school. It's not racism. And the amount of money they spend on booze, there's none left to feed the kids. They are one big family, the whole community of members. Hygiene can be a problem. What if I told you that some of them confused the toilet bowl with the sink? Sometimes ten or more live in one house, somebody dies there and they all move out, never to live there again. The housing money has gone out the window."

"How about the stolen generation?" I interrupt.

"Let's face reality here, look at the practical side. As sad as it was, they were the first well-educated generation of Aborigines that could wash, tidy up, and find a job. My point is we're here to stay. We're not going anywhere now, are we? We're one. So they had better get used to it because now they can't walk it alone any more."

45
Welcome and Piss Off: On How to Find and Not to Lose

We're back at the restaurant.

"What is that shit?" asks the spooky hulk in the boiler suit, who has seen the stew with dumplings while passing through the kitchen again. He pulls a yucky face. "Gimme a meat pie," then he's gone.

After the dinner, it's time for some drinks and we move to the local pub. Greg and Brenda go home. They invite us later to their dogout house. We sit with Joey and Amy, his fiancée.

"Do you know why there is so much sex in Coober Pedy?" says Joey in a bored voice.

"No."

45 Welcome and Piss Off: On How to Find and Not to Lose

"Beaches everywhere but no water."

Sex on the Beach is Midori, plus vodka, plus Bacardi, plus Bailey's. There is the Squashed Frog: Midori, Advocaat Liqueur, plus a bit of Grenadine syrup with raspberry juice. And the Centipede. Kahlua, Bailey's, Grenadine syrup.

"Coober is not very safe," he goes on. "There used to be about thirty people in my class, now there's only about half of them. The rest went nuts. Like, some of them surfed—did you know you can surf here? You just get an old loose car bonnet and tow it behind your car for blokes to jump on. Full throttle. Add a bit of gambling in your spare time, drugs, and you're screwed. What else can you do here? Not many girls. The nearest, like, normal township is Adelaide, 850 kilometres away. I'm going there in five days. You can come with me."

"We have to get out tomorrow," I say.

Dugout church in Coober Pedy, SA[45]

The subject changes to opals. "If you grow up here, you develop

45 Dugout churches in Coober Pedy, SA https://goo.gl/maps/K4vA64kepsG2

an eye for it. It's never just a clean, shiny stone lying on the ground, waiting for you. You see a tiny tip that looks almost exactly like all the rocks around it, dirty and grey. Often it's not even a stone. It's a mussel. But they are worth more. You can find thousands of dollars like that. I once found one that's worth sixteen thousand. Wait a minute!"

Before we say anything he hops into his car and disappears.

We look around. The pub is chock-a-block, which means full to the last seat. The party at the next table is having a heated bogan debate.

"*—yooooooouu're a fucking legend mate, aren't ya?*" one of them exclaims.

"*Mate, you have noooo idea, have ya? HAVE YA? NO—FUCK-ING—IDEA, moron!*" the other retorts, then starts to explain something in language too fast for us to understand. But not for long.

"*FUCK OFF!*" The first one cuts in, as if not wanting to listen any more. Then they all burst into a long, uncontrollable fit of laughter.

Joey is back in ten minutes. The opal looks exactly like a mussel, except it's all blue with flickering colours. So we truly are on the seabed.

"Once you find an opal, you think you'll find it again. And so you search and search. It's like a slot machine. Like gambling. I knew a guy who found three hundred thousand worth of opals. In six months he didn't have enough money to change his tyre."

The pub starts to pulsate. Young and not so young, all start to sing and dance.

We're staying in the underground camp tonight but we've no idea how to get there.

To us, all the rubble piles outside look exactly the same.

"I'll get you there. Don't you worry," shouts Joey.

Joey's phone rings. We're going to Greg's. Amy goes home.

*

Greg's dugout is like an underground castle. It's got at least five large rooms and he says he's going to dig out more when he runs out of space.

"This place is for the strong. Wimps won't hold. You have to show your muscle sometimes. A neighbour of mine used to tip rubbish next to my ventilation shaft, making compost. Terrible pong was coming in the house with every blast of wind. Rotten stuff.

"I asked him all the time, nice and polite, begging him to remove it. Na! He didn't care. So I took a dead bird and hung it down his shaft. In a few days the stink disappeared. He got the message.

"Or look at people who noodle on others' lots. You spend thousands for preparation, and then some lout from a city somewhere touches down on your sandpit to sponge off your work." He speaks about leases further afield; only potch is found in the town now.

"They're risking their own arse, I'm telling you. The first shot is in the air. From time to time, somebody gets clubbed or shot. But that's the insiders. Outside tourists, like you, who behave, can take it easy. If you want to live here, you need to earn respect. And to pay respect."

We're trying his home-made cognacs and whiskeys. They are very good, and he explains the process. If they were poured from an original bottle, we wouldn't know the difference. Greg is incredibly versatile. One minute he can talk about bootlegging, then change to the innards of a car engine, and just few minutes later he shows he is also well versed in the greatest classical music composers of the nineteenth century.

At half past twelve, Joey's phone rings again. Amy has cut her finger badly, opening a fruit can. She is as pale as a ghost when we arrive, but luckily, an ambulance is not necessary.

Joey sits slumped on a chair, tired. We all are.

"Forget the underground camp. Just stay in my house," he says finally, two minutes before falling asleep.

*

Greg's noodling machinery is on the other side of the town and is in full swing the next day. He gave us directions on how to get there, but they're not clear. Once past the town, it's easy to get lost[46]. Mounds of dirt and more mounds of dirt, one next to another, for kilometres without an end. Greg has an excavator he uses to scoop large chunks of earth and then load onto a conveyor belt—another machine—where he separates rocks from better pieces like potch, gypsum and hopefully opal. The rest of the dirt is spewed out of the machine, making another big mound next to it.

Excavator loads dirt onto a conveyor belt ...

Anything other than dirt stands out on the belt like shiny spots in the dark room, where he spends some time and then reappears with a bucketful of carefully selected debris. Most of it, like potch, is completely worthless and you would have to get a few tonnes of

46 It is easy to get lost outside the town of Coober Pedy, SA https://goo.gl/maps/EUPtbdmzke22

gypsum to make any money at all, but he throws it in anyway. Just in case. He will examine it under daylight or later at home. He does a few cycles like that and then prescribes himself a break.

... then it's sifted in the dark room

"See, this is my lot. You have to have a permit before you start to … oh shit—!" He has just remembered something and quickly leaves. I am not sure whether to follow him or wait. He stands by one of the marking posts and overwrites something with a permanent marker and a piece of rag. "I forgot it expired yesterday."

Sifting machinery[47] in full swing

"There! You see, it's all about trying. There are days and days

---
47 Sifting machinery in Coober Pedy, SA https://goo.gl/maps/LTTGfnPrmru

when you find bugger-all but then, in a single stroke of luck, you can find a few thousand dollars. The last one I found was a fossil. The best you can do then is to hide it in a good safe and keep your mouth shut until you sell it. You're not going to put on public display in a local pub."

We're thinking about Joey. Whoops.

Alex and Sumio stand by the Orthodox Church dugout in Coober Pedy. Each time we see them, we plunge into a combination of pity and admiration of their strong will.

Another rest place is Bon Bon, about 200 kilometres south. It's quite cold now but one of my legs starts swelling—a delayed tropical skin rash. It's only going to be sorted by a doctor in Melbourne. Bon Bon on the Stuart Highway is good for having a rest and not much more. It's only a dot in the midst of barren land. It's not far from the road, and the dry tree limbs and roots will do to make a fire. A hot meal saves the day. We realise that somewhere around the Red Centre we lost warm nights. The difference in temperature at day and night is significant now.

Two headlights are coming near from the other direction. Backpackers going north. They put up their tent and join us at the fireplace, making *damper*, simple bread from self-rising flour and water baked in the fire ash or on a stick. We can tell them what's ahead and they can tell us.

46
Firecracker Town: Woomera

All the dried-up Lake Hart can offer is a car wreck of a small van and thousands of annoying flies. And a perfect backdrop for a picture. Its silver, salty bed shows marks of what once used to be a jetty, a long row of wooden dots gnawed by time and weather.

Woomera, not far from here, is an interesting end to the South Australian opal territory.

46 Firecracker Town: Woomera

It is a purpose-built town, used to be closed to the public, and was used as a military base for soldiers and scientists working on rocket programs. From the air it would look like a small suburb in the middle of a desert. It was designed during the Cold War to test long-range ballistic missiles. It's a gate to "nowhere". To add insult to injury, the governments in the fifties used this and other Aboriginal lands for nuclear programs, even having a few testing blasts in places like Maralinga and Emu.

Right after the last street, thousands of kilometres of barren land starts and the ramp that used to fire the rockets got its name from Aboriginal spear-thrower: Woomera. There are few people now, mainly employees of the local museum. It nostalgically reminds of those "glorious" times.

Rocket park in Woomera,[48] SA

Today's administration is more sophisticated. If there is a research station somewhere, it will be well hidden from public sight, thousands of kilometres even from here.

In the nineties, Woomera found a new use as a refugee detention centre. During riots in 2000, about five hundred refugees went in the streets, protests were quashed, but later the facility packed up and took it somewhere else.

---
48 Rocket park in Woomera https://goo.gl/maps/uGkX9ZbEsUy

An older Australian told me the other day that he never knew what side of the road a car would come from. The American Jeeps didn't bother driving on the left side, sometimes going on the left, sometimes on the right, depending on their mood. It used to be a government domain and probably still is. The town is just waiting for a new opportunity.

There are about thirty-five days left and five and a half thousand kilometres to conquer.

VII. Port Augusta to Melbourne

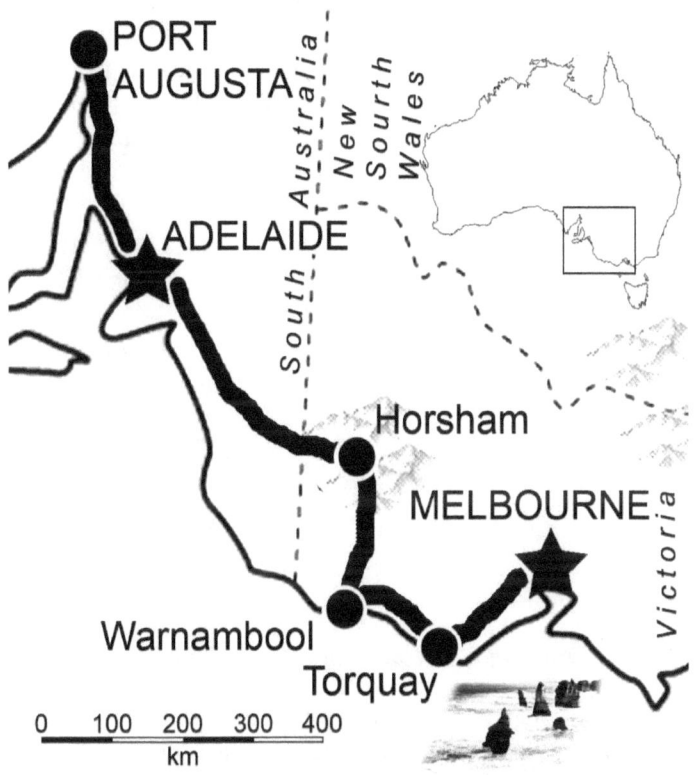

47

Tough Luck Mountains: Ikara-Flinders Ranges

Port Augusta is where the soul of one Australia more or less ends and another one begins: more civilised, slightly more inhabited and coastal. Up until now, the itinerary was relatively simple. One way: south. Now this road will fork out into dozens of options.

The outback is actually one huge elevation without mountains—a dry plateau, positioned moderately above sea level with rather unfriendly winds steadily blowing across it. Shortly before Port Augusta,[49] this plateau gives way to a gradual descent to the coast. We're going down as if from hills which are not there. A place called Lake Hart is the beginning of one of the largest drainage basins in the world: Lake Eyre. It is also the only place in Australia that is actually below sea level. If the climate so desires, the water capacity of the area is larger than a few European countries combined, but most of the time it's dry.

Dried up Lake Hart: Part of Lake Eyre basin,[50] SA

Port Augusta is still a small town—a foray into Adelaide, which in itself is not too large. City life in the true sense is still far away. One knows that from looking at the cars. The shiny city darlings are nowhere to be seen, and there are only the more robust breed of mainly four-wheel drives or their shabby-looking two-wheel cousins like ours, with remnants of red dust over their number plates. Large trucks pass us in both directions, even one carrying a whole house like a giant "snail" with two little flashing car "ants", one in front and the second in rear, holding the Oversize sign. We have to stop and make way. Not far from here to the north-west and on our left, there are some of the most extraordinary land-

---

49 Road to Port Augusta with Flinders Ranges in the background, SA https://goo.gl/maps/sY7NXvA3nBC2
50 Lake Hart, SA: beginning of a huge drainage basin https://goo.gl/maps/ue15NfBwrww

47 Tough Luck Mountains: Ikara-Flinders Ranges

scapes of Australia, a range that might just as well be tagged the "tough luck" mountains—the Flinders Ranges, originally known as Ikara.

Road to Ikara-Flinders Ranges, SA

Matthew Flinders was actually the guy who most vigorously advocated "Australia" for its official name, but his legacy is somehow lost among the accomplishments of his more famous contemporaries. He was six years in prison on Mauritius, he was wrecked on reefs in Queensland when sailing back home to England; while he survived, he lost all his possessions including his precious diaries—and he died at only forty years old. Yet he managed to circumnavigate Australia and map it.

As far as fate is concerned, "his" ranges are ... a little bit like him. They were largely settled by pioneers from northern Europe, mainly country people and farmers. The scenario was repeated many times. Each year at Christmas, the humble families would sit around their tables in quiet obedience, praying to God for rain, to at last irrigate their thirsty land, feed their cows, bring better crops, and generally improve their livelihoods. They prayed in their first year. Nothing. They prayed in their second year. Nothing again. They were praying for a few more years. And still nothing. And then the rain came. It came and stayed for long enough to flood the area and ruin everything they had built in all those years.

VII. Port Augusta to Melbourne

Ruins left behind by settlers in Ikara-Flinders Ranges, SA

There was even a decent rail track linking the local towns; steam trains today known as Pichi Richi that give a good taste of what it looked like in those times.

The long straight road to Flinders Ranges is like going back to the past. There are many empty stone house foundations where families once lived, and all this with the backdrop of the magnificent hills behind them. Its original name *Ikara* remembers much more. A touch of magic.

One of such eerie places is Wilpena Pound[51]—a hill formation that from high above looks like a meteor crater, but is actually an ancient seabed. It used to be called *Adnyamathanha* by the Aborigines, meaning "meeting place". Later the farmers wanted to take advantage of it as a natural enclosure for cattle herds, but Mother Nature thought better of it. With one extreme to another, it drove them away with no remorse. And so they left their homes behind. We are only lucky they didn't build them with today's fibro building standards. There would be nothing left.

Frost forms on our tent in the morning, combining perfectly with the rising sun. The campground is comfortable, even with

---

51 Wilpena Pound, SA that looks like meteor crater https://goo.gl/maps/vnyt-V7Zj9r42

music in the toilets. We're hiking on St Mary Peak—or Ngarri Mudlanha[52] —the highest peak of Flinders Ranges at 1,171 metres above sea level.

Wilpena Pound "crater", SA: View from St Mary Peak

Not much, one might say, but it's five hours of a full-attention walk. Parts of the "crater" can be observed from above, and the top is covered with large rock plates with cliffs and steep falls. A currawong bird greets us there with its typical ominous sound. Throw a bit of bread down the abyss and it knows exactly where it fell, so good and sharp is his sight.

St Mary Peak/Ngarri Mudlanha, SA: 1,171 m ASL

The picturesque scenery ends back in Port Augusta, where the

---

52 St Mary Peak in Flinders Ranges https://goo.gl/maps/Ftrt2XSw3bF2

more inhabited Australia begins, although it is not nearly as populous as we initially expected.

48
Adelaide in a Nutshell

The world's biggest rocking horse, in Gumeracha on the northeast slopes of Adelaide, is a tall structure in front of a toy factory and another one of the Australian "biggies collection". The smell of coffee and freshly worked wood is just too irresistible.

Big Rocking Horse in Gumeracha, SA[53]

The road from Port Augusta to Adelaide goes through a rolling landscape, and we're here at a time when everything is lushly green among the farmhouses, vineyards and fields.

Adelaide is the only Australian city that predominantly used sandstone and brick as building materials because wood was in short supply. The tram to Glenelg, the beach part, feels a bit like Vienna.

South Australia is the driest state, the government is its largest employer, and there are only about one and a half million people. Only about ten percent of people live outside the capital.

---
53 Big rocking horse in Gumeracha https://goo.gl/maps/6ftT7vBYk1q

For now we don't need to know more because we're only in transit here anyway.

This time a transit to prehistoric times.

49
Fifty Thousand Years Ago: Naracoorte

The South Australian town of Naracoorte is surrounded by agricultural land, and at first sight there seems to be nothing interesting here[54]. Victoria is around the corner, but because they discovered something amazingly weird in this place, something that can only be seen here, it's not the right time to cross the border yet.

Diprotodon optatum was one of the largest marsupials that ever lived on the planet. It was a wombat-beast as big as grizzly, but instead of tearing its victim apart with sharp teeth, it would rather stash it in its giant pouch and chew on it later. A giant hamster. On close examining the size of its jaw, it might comfortably fit a person with backpack and a camera on tripod.

The giant wombat: Naracoorte Caves National Park

---

54 Naracoorte Caves National Park https://goo.gl/maps/eBDG7f6KqNM2

Procoptodon goliah, for a change, was a gigantic kangaroo. It was about two to three metres tall and it weighed about two hundred kilos. I don't want to think what that mass could do to a car in a front collision. It is well known, however, that very strange creatures used to live in this part of South Australia, and this was, in eternity terms, not so long ago: only some fifty thousand years back. Marsupial lions with terrible, large tusks, huge koalas, at least twenty kangaroo types of scary proportions, and many other rather unpronounceable species.

Their demise, interestingly enough, coincides with the first traces of humans' existence on the continent. They probably didn't leave voluntarily. Humans are said to have helped them on their way out, with their systematic killing and burning their food.

There are many caves in Australia, but this particular one, with a museum at its front, is heritage-listed. Bats live here: not the much-hated macrochiroptera that feeds on fruit, but the microchiroptera that uses ultrasound for navigation. They live in complete darkness. Tourists visit them regularly with their thermal auras sending thousands of micro particles of sweat, cheap clothing, street dust, and breath vapours into the cave walls. As an American tourist pointed out to me as a joke once, "If the cave walls are not green enough, the cave makes too little money." But this cave seems to be managed responsibly. They don't beam any light inside because there are tiny insects the bats are dependent on. If the insects die, the bats die too.

"Whoops," whispers our friend, who is showing us around and is with us in the cave. "We used to camp and sing with a guitar in here when we were young."

We're going to a farm, where we will stay with people we had met in Ormiston Gorge. Naracoorte is not just a piece of history. Good wines are produced here, although not as famous as the neighbouring Barossa Valley. Vineyards of known brands are glimmering on the side of the narrow road as we go along. There are massive trees along that road. At one of them, a sign is attached about a young backpacker girl who was killed here in a car accident. She was driving to work and had a front collision with a truck.

Our friends Ben and Heather have a farm with two thousand sheep. Sometimes they have to move them around to their other property ten kilometres from the house. Moving the herd takes all day and they do it on foot. We drive there on the next day and it's a large open space with plenty of stumps all over. A large black magpie is squawking nearby with a malicious sound. A hyena-bird, as they put it. When a sheep needs to give birth and tips over to the ground, it can peck out its eyes. Luckily, we don't see that, but one animal misfortune does happen later that day. The sheep are being counted in their enclosures when one of them freaks out and breaks her leg against the metal fencing. That equals a suicide because she has to be slaughtered right after. She must have known where she was heading: into the nearby meat processing plant. But the farmer doesn't like killing his own sheep. We can see and feel it.

His sheep dog is a skilled champion. He puts up a real show, jumping on the sheep's backs knowing exactly whether to go left or right, after only a slight change of voice pitch.

We're over the border in Victoria and camp at Mount Arapiles that night. A perfect quiet place, good for a rest by the fire and even greater for traditional climbers. They look like tiny dots on the rocky hill opposite our tent. Although we don't know it yet, it is a nice prelude to something even more fascinating. The name we'd not yet heard still firmly resonates in our ears. The Grampians.

50
All Seasons in One Day: Grampians

Only a few days ago, I thought that nothing could be as remote as the outback. I didn't know we would drive to a place called Chimney Pots. It's complete solitude. The Grampians is a crazy mountain range, not only in weather patterns, but also in the character of its tracks.

But first we're heading to Stawell, which is our first gate to the national park. We're staying with our friends Jim and Sarah. They have a nice little house, an adolescent daughter who doesn't say hello, and an old dog who unwittingly walks through rooms, bumps to furniture and regularly marches into a fireplace. And in between his yowling episodes, Jim is asking whether we've heard about a "nerve test". No, we haven't. Apparently there is a spot in the park—a rock protrusion—that can really check your nerves, he says. The problem is we can't find it on the maps.

"You'll see it, it's a well-known place."

So the next day we go to Halls Gap,[55] which is the real gate to the park.

Hail in Silent Street: Grampians/Gariwerd

The creek water is the brownish colour of beer on *Wonderland*

---

[55] A gate to the Grampians: Halls Gap https://goo.gl/maps/fdJDy3grmg42

Walk, which goes from *Grand Canyon* uphill[56]. The subsequent trail leads through a little forest to a narrow path between two rock walls. There are ladders and the gully is called *Silent Street.* It was nice and sunny down at the car park, but we have hail falling on our heads, and it quickly changes into snowflakes. It's the first time we see snow in Australia and it comes as surprise. But the Grampians—also known as Gariwerd—is like that. All seasons can meet in one day.

The stony path is very slippery, and a fast-moving fog greets us at the top. On finally reaching the spot called the Pinnacle, there is a little snowstorm.

The guy at the information centre didn't want to tell us where the nerve test was. He was all shilly-shallying before admitting "it was not advertised any more". It's actually a few hundred metres from the Pinnacle, but common sense kicks in and refuses to do it.

We are soaked wet going through the Grampians Gardens, back to the Wonderland Car Park and then driving to Stawell again, to a nice fireplace with the poor old doggy continuing his sad canine geriatric *danse macabre*. He must have burned his muzzle at least a hundred times now.

"Do you know Hollow Mountain?" Jim starts again. And he hands me a book where "Mount Stapylton to Hollow Mountain" is dubbed the most beautiful track in Australia. But there is a trick. The book is from the 80s. We are used to modern tourist guides that make the tracks twice as long and three times as slow, always thinking of the "weakest link" in the chain and how satisfy everybody. A just in case approach. And this book says the track is only five kilometres long but it takes five hours. And we're laughing at it. What bullshit!

But it isn't.

---

[56] Cliffs of the Grampians https://goo.gl/maps/5ChNpz1KyYo

VII. Port Augusta to Melbourne

51
What Guides Won't Say: Real Peaks of Grampians

The starting point to Mount Stapylton is on the north-east side of the park. From Stawell it's half-way to Horsham, passing the Giant Koala[57] and turning left to get to Mount Zero Picnic Area[58]. That's our point zero. Most people will pass it because they're too keen on getting to the heart of the park and will never know the best part.

Giant Koala, VIC

Mount Stapylton to Hollow Mountain deserves to be named one of the most adrenalin-filled tracks in Australia; it's very tough and it officially doesn't exist. The park authorities pretend it's not there. It's a typical example of how the blame game has changed the Australian hiking mentality.

The weather, as already said, is treacherous and can catch even the experienced hikers off guard. Only a few months ago, people got lost on an otherwise ordinary walking path and their rescue took three days. They were still alive but had bad hypothermia. These mountains are not high but very rough and steep. This track

---
57 Giant Koala https://goo.gl/maps/EbV7HHc2wUP2
58 Mount Zero Picnic Area https://goo.gl/maps/CVroDzRQxKr

in particular is not for the faint-hearted. There are many places where it's easy to fall—and far.

The first part to Mount Stapylton is still on the map and is easy. It goes slightly uphill along a massive rock platform until it reaches a remarkable natural sculpture called Bird Rock, because it looks like a large squatting bird. The track becomes steeper from this point, and after about twenty minutes the surrounding rocks become slightly confusing. Sometimes it's not quite clear where to go. We cling to the trail that goes left and try to get up to where it officially ends: Mount Stapylton.

Bird rock: Mount Stapylton

Wind blows at the top and an interesting view opens up. The "bird" can be spotted down from the cliff and all around us is a chaos of rock formations. They are somehow arranged into three large discernible ridges on the map—a labyrinth that it is rather hard to find the way through. The trick is to find an opening in the rock at the end of the track that spirals down about five metres through the rock mass, which is the path back to car park.

Mount Stapylton to Hollow Mountain, VIC

After five minutes, we're lost. The detailed description doesn't help. It's all going downhill in all directions, first slowly, then steeper so that we can't see over the horizon how far it actually goes. Putting backpacks aside, we search for the most plausible way for a good thirty minutes, a few times returning to the same place. After quite an effort and mental strain, we slowly manage to get down a rockslide, to find no abyss but a track that goes further. It's been well hidden from sight all that time. We try to keep up the rocky path and never to go too low. If we descend too much, it means we are on the wrong path. There are high rock chimneys at one stage, but the way forward is hidden again. We find a used karabiner lying on the ground. It's a popular rock climbing spot. Sometimes we lie down and admire the long steep walls around us, to calm down. There are a few places between the ridges where the rock is split by a narrow but very long and deep crack. We have to cross them at the highest point, because rarely is there a less scary way around.

51 What Guides Won't Say: Real Peaks of Grampians

Suddenly voices come from behind. Two young guys from Melbourne with a slightly better map and surprise on their faces, saying they "didn't expect anything like that". The next crack, however, is even longer. It's split open for the full length of the ridge. It's more than clear now than somewhere we'll have to step over it. The gap is smallest at the highest point. The fact that it's already afternoon and there are heavy clouds forming over our heads is not taking off stress. A jump is out of the question. There is nowhere to land. We cross slowly and carefully.

Walls of Mount Stapylton

A large natural atrium is next, with a big fallen tree in its middle. We find a few ways out but they are all blind. We're losing precious time again, and again: we didn't take a torch in case it gets dark. As if we didn't make that mistake before.

Only few cracks lead out of the atrium. Managing to get through one of the narrower ones, we're out, on the outside rock surface again. Trying to keep as high on the crest as possible, we get to a place where there is no way forward. The vertical wall of another ridge is opposite, and every direction from where we stand runs steeply down. That's the other side of the track, because now, we're on the other peak called Hollow Mountain. It's time to find the rock opening. There are four of us and we search for about half an hour. Nature was playing a trick because it is on the other side, well hidden from the way we chose.

Hollow Mountain, the Grampians, VIC

Spiralling down to safety after a few hours' walk, we only now get talking to our co-hikers. Where we come from, what we saw, and this place—how it's going to stick.

"So, what's your name?" I ask, after introducing myself at last.

"David," says the first one.

"He is David *Lynch*," says the other one with a grin.

"Okay, beautiful. And that thing behind us was the *Twin Peaks*. Great."

"Nice to meet you!"

52
Clay and Whales: Great Ocean Road

We farewell Stawell by looking at its gold mine. Heavy trucks with funny flattened cabins disappear into an entrance in the ground that leads kilometres under the surface. They re-emerge from another opening with haul beds full of dirt, tip the load and off they go again. The golden bench we sit on represents the amount of gold the mine has yielded in all its existence. That's it. Just one cuboid shape you can sit on.

Beautiful green landscapes, populated with thousands of sheep, extend from here to the coast and the Victorian pride called the Great Ocean Road. Warrnambool is where we start. We're in time to watch whales. They come every year around September and they show off their huge fins and bellies only a few hundred metres from the shore. When you're patient enough for it to come out of water a bit more, you realise how enormous this animal really is.

The rugged coast can be fully appreciated from certain spots. It's not rocky, but formed from a very hard clay. A few places might even be dangerous. To get back up from the water after a fall from this place would be totally impossible.

The London Bridge,[59] about seventy kilometres from Warrnambool, used to be—as its name suggests—a bridge, but in 1990 it collapsed and stranded a couple of people on what became an island with no bridge to the other side. Lucky for them, they'd already crossed it when it went down. They wouldn't have survived otherwise. In a bit of shock, they were rescued by a helicopter a few hours later.

This coast is also famous for large number of wrecked ships, most of them from the nineteenth century, when many first settlers sadly died. After about eight months of sea voyage, and almost at destination, they were looking forward to the shore; but that same shore tore them apart. That's why from Moonlight Head

---
59 London Bridge at Great Ocean Road, Victoria https://goo.gl/maps/YCmntp-mE2os

to Port Fairy it's called Shipwreck Coast. About eighty ships were doomed here.

London Bridge, rough Victorian coast[60]

What's interesting is that some of those ships could have been wrecked well before the nineteenth century, and so were not necessarily English but possibly Portuguese, but these are only speculations as no evidence was found. If found, it would rewrite history books.

The Twelve Apostles[61] are not twelve but rather eight or so. Never mind. Some of them will collapse and new ones will emerge over time. A long time. In the meantime, the creative name attracts thousands in bus tours. More trivial names were considered, like Sow and Piglets, but the current name did extremely well. A touch of genius. The winding road along the coast is worth every inch. It's rather cold in the Cumberland River Holiday Park, seven kilometres from Lorne, but there is a beautifully whispering river by an outside fireplace. Torquay is Great Ocean Road's end station. Wild sea lashes its beaches and is therefore a respected surfing venue. One of its kind in Australia. The "capital of surf", according to locals.

---

60 Rough Victorian coast https://goo.gl/maps/YKMXwYeQ8Bt
61 A Victorian icon: Twelve Apostles https://goo.gl/maps/TYF2D7oFTex

Big city life can be smelled from here now. It's Geelong that heralds something even bigger. We clean the car from mud and dust because we're only one step away from Melbourne.

53
Melbourne in a Nutshell

Our first thoughts in Melbourne were those of replacing the window I had to smash in Kakadu a few thousand kilometres back, and healing the tropical infection on my leg. I also call scrapyards around town. The window is somewhere out there, and for a fair price. Once I show up, however, the price tag goes up mysteriously. Remembering the Greg's words in Coober Pedy, I have to insist on the agreed price or I'll turn and go somewhere else. It works. As for the infection, it was fixed by pills.

We spend some time in second-hand bookstores in Russel, Bourke, and Brunswick Streets, the soul of the city. It's a nice atmosphere, with a reputation for being drug intersections. Melbourne feels worldly. Coffee shops rather than clubs, trams rather than buses, and the down-to-earth attitudes of people make it so, and for a while it's excused for being just another thumping conglomerate. A bit Italian, a tad Greek, and that's where I stop because I am not a bloody city guide. Where we go for dinner, there is a poster on the wall. Chopper is giving an evening show.

54
Uncle Chopper And Papa Rog

Although most Australians like to think of themselves as normal, civilised people today, often the first mental image that strikes many overseas visitors are their ancestors in chains being hauled up on a wooden ship somewhere in England. The ex-penal-colony stigma is still alive and kicking, all in the context of: yeah, yeah, they did wrong, were deservedly sent to the furthest known tip of this world to work their way back to society, but at the same time we'll never see or hear of them again because it's so bloody far (chuckle, chuckle). Weren't the English forefathers clever? Two birds killed with one stone, as it were.

Meeting this kind of a criminal archetype in person, however, might be more easily said than done. Criminals in today's Australia look just like their counterparts overseas: indiscernible from normal citizenry.

And that's why the pub in one of the suburbs is packed to bursting. There are more artefacts on display tonight.

Mark Brandon Chopper Read, who once terrorised the underbelly of Melbourne, will always be known as a celebrity. Being an upgraded, heavyweight version of the now largely obsolete Ned Kelly, Chopper is a glorified villain and the main star of the evening.

True, he didn't eat seven compatriots like Alexander Pierce back in 1822, but it doesn't mean the times have gone any sissier. He famously had his ears cut off and became the central character of a successful movie. After serving his time, he became a hyped book author, selling a substantial number of copies, and he even wrote a spooky children's book.

His forerunner, a skinny type who looks like a host of a sleazy bogan program, whose name I don't remember, takes to picking on the audience right from the start.

"What's your name, sir? Justin? Do you know why girls love you, Justin? Because they love you just in.

"And are there any fucking Pommies tonight? What are you sir?

Some voices come from the audience.

"—yeah, like Polish? Never heard that in my life! Hard-core sense of humour you have over there, eh? And you?"

"Czech."

"Check what?"

"Czech Republic."

"Wh—What? Really?"

A moment of silence.

"Any—any other fucking Republics? Banana Republic anyone? Are you still dropping bombs on each other or you laid down your arms now?"

After a twenty-minute monologue, he introduces a guest. We have never seen him before. He is a decent-looking "uncle" with a nice cordial smile. He is clean-shaven and his name is Roger something Rogerson.

"Have you ever seen anybody with legs as skinny as that?" giggles the no-name host. He sits on a stool with his microphone in his hand as if he is about to start telling children's stories. A bit disappointing for a show like that, we're thinking. This guy looks like he's just leaving for Sunday church.

"Ladies and gentlemen, a warm welcome for Dodger!" Audience applauding.

His first story is about a criminal who went on prison leave and was expected to make a move on a sports club. Dodger's party was waiting for him, and arrested him so convincingly that his head disappeared from his shoulders and his mother had to identify him by a curved toe.

"Nice lady, she really was. I felt sorry for her. I tried to cheer her up: if your son had gone by the protocol, nothing would have happened to him. He had signed a form asking if he was planning to commit any crimes while on leave."

The most notorious guy Dodger had finished off was Warren Lanfranchi—a drug dealer from Sydney. He shot him dead in the street, point blank, and was acquitted because it was "self-defence". Lanfranchi's girlfriend, a prostitute, Sallie-Anne Huckstepp didn't buy the story and turned it into a media circus, almost becoming a star until she was found dead in a Centennial Park pond in Sydney's Eastern Suburbs. They never found out who had done it and Dodger got a bravery award. He used to head a police hold-up squad in his famous days, and had been a highly regarded cop.

"I got a tip-off from our guy, leading me to a young fellow who had been getting around raping children around Petersham. I sorted him out with my gun, but unfortunately he was a son of a police official who ranked higher than I did at the time, and he gave me a hard time for ever after."

He offers a moral to the story. "Then one day I found he'd finally died. I went to his funeral and when everybody was gone, I pissed all over his grave."

Dodger only went to jail after he had—kind of—botched the shooting of his rival police officer. His pals didn't do it right. He says he's always looked up to his work mates who made millions drug trafficking. He was never anywhere near it. He was famously released after serving a year or so, and he'd be successfully dodging until this day, had he not forgotten, some time later in 2014, that in this new age of technology, surveillance cameras were virtually everywhere, and they would record him if he's trying to get rid of a corpse in a storage unit. Completely underestimating the investigative skills of his younger colleagues "by trade", he and his buddy, another ex-cop, didn't go to great lengths to clean their tracks after the murder of a young drug trafficker. With that, he finally embraced jail as his permanent home: in 2016, he is sentenced to life. Of course, when we sit in the pub and listen to his stories, we don't know that yet.

Next, there is an auction. There are items for sale, all signed by Chopper, who we still haven't seen after two-thirds of the program. A four-kilo axe, signed by Chopper, a large butcher knife signed by Chopper, colour posters of Chopper sitting on a chopper signed by Chopper, an authentic photograph of the dead Turk who Chopper shot in the eye in the final scene of the movie, after being led for execution to the wrong car park. Also signed by Chopper.

54 Uncle Chopper And Papa Rog

"Come on, pussies! Don't make this hard!" the host says. "Just think of the huge resale potential of these memorabilia!"

The highlight of the evening has finally arrived. Chopper himself with a beer can in his hand.

"Well, first of all, the movie isn't true, it's eighty per cent true but twenty per cent fucking bullshit. I've never beaten up my girlfriend like that and her name was not Tanya. I was never a shill like I was portrayed in the movie. That wouldn't work. I wouldn't have gotten away with something like that. Anyway, I'm lucky I'm still alive." He drinks beer.

"Where was I. Oh, yeah, I was gonna tell you how they chopped off my ears. That was brutally true in the movie. The whole prison had turned against me and I wouldn't live long if I didn't do something, right? And I had to show them I was mad enough to justify transfer because they said I wasn't going anywhere! And what's better than chopping your own ears off to prove your point, right? One of my mates was doing it, while others were watching, and when he was halfway through the first ear, I felt this warm water trickling down my neck, except it wasn't water, it was blood, right? I said to him, 'What the fuck are you doing?' And he says, 'I'm trying to be gentle, mate'. And I say to him, calmly, that if he's hacking my fucking ear off, he can't do it gently like that, because it fucking hurts! It hurts like hell! And so he did the other one real quick."

He drinks beer.

"Yeah, when they cut your ears, there's blood everywhere. Tarantino fucked that all up in his *Reservoir Dogs*. There wasn't a single drop of blood. He should have consulted me, I'm a fucking ear-chopping authority, ain't I? I chopped my ears off well before anybody even had bloody heard of Tarantino."

He drinks beer.

"And they didn't even invite me to the screening, though it was all about me. Bana called me and said if I wasn't going, he wasn't going, but all the others didn't want me there because they knew

191

if I was there all the journos would stay clear of them, cos they'd all be around *me*, right? And I didn't make a fucking cent from the movie. They ripped me off! They would get their hands on it anyway, so I just transferred the dough to fucking children's hospitals, but then I had second thoughts and politely asked them to pay it back, but I tell you, you don't fuck with children's hospitals. Don't even try it. But no hard feelings. I do like children. Really do."

He drinks beer.

"Do you want to ask me anything?"

"How do you like your imitators, like Ronnie Johns. He does it right, doesn't he—?" somebody asks from the crowd.

"This guy's a wanker. I don't talk like Ronnie Johns, do I? That's not my voice, the speed, is it?" He makes some gestures.

"I bumped into him once and I told him, 'If you want to be like me, chop your ears off, mate, have the guts, otherwise you'll always be a fake.'"

He drinks beer.

"Another question?"

"Would you say anything to the film-makers if you met them in the street?" somebody from the crowd asks.

"Yeah, where is me fucking money, ya bastards!"

Chopper died in 2013.

VIII. Melbourne to Sydney

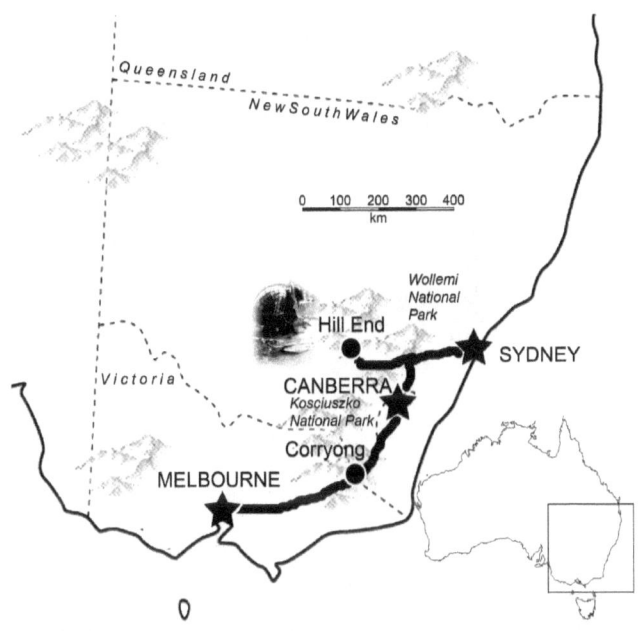

55
Mister Ricketts' Beautiful Soul

If we wanted, we could be in Sydney in one day now. But we prefer the roads less travelled and stretch it for three more weeks. Pure chance gets us to the Dandenong Ranges, east of Melbourne, where a true sanctuary can be found. William Ricketts dedicated his entire life to clay sculptures. This is a place of tranquillity, mystique and meditation[62]. He wanted it that way, low-key, he was not one for publicity. A winding road leads us there with local produce for sale, such as honey or flowers, all in unattended stalls: just throw your money in the box and we're set. The price list is

[62] William Ricketts Sanctuary, Victoria https://goo.gl/maps/Lqbot3kHsUA2

standing next to it. When we enter a small enclosure disguised in the greenery of the surrounding wood, we enter another world, one that has little in common with the world outside.

Kingdom of peace

The entrance is guarded by two well-built Aboriginal leaders on big boulders, and all around the garden there are faces, busts, hands, and body shapes. Here is a character peeking out of a tree, there is another stepping out of a stone, they crawl in and out of their rocky ambience, all in perfect harmony with their surroundings. There are warriors, mothers, children, and all their faces have the smallest details, showing strong emotions, some of them quite chilling.

Ricketts transcended into Aboriginal soul. At least, that's what he felt towards the end of his life. He talks about his visions from a small TV screen. He bought this land in 1920s and named it Potter's Sanctuary. He worked on it all life and this is his legacy: a lush, green, kind kingdom of beaming energy, mystery and silence.

We borrow a bit of that energy and head over the hills to the High Country, along the same winding road that brought us here.

56
North Over the Hill Country

When going north from Victoria to New South Wales, it's either Australian highway —called a motorway here—or Australian countryside. We opt for country and head for Wangaratta, where we stay with friends who live in a house on the quiet hillside. There is something special about walking around this beautiful landscape knowing so few people are in the area. They also have dogs, and so we see our first echidna in the wild. The dogs sniffed it up and it is tucked into the ground so that only the few top spikes are sticking out. Mount Buffalo is not far from here—a Victorian Alpine National Park. Snow chains are mandatory for all conventional cars in September and we're risking a fine. Back in the city it didn't occur to me we might ever need them. They are expensive, the weather is perfectly dry and we're only passing. Given this situation, we decide it's overkill.

Colac Colac near Corryong is the last stop in Victoria, then the mountain pass takes us to Australia's "first state". New South Wales.

Typical mountain road, Victoria/NSW border

The border to New South Wales is on Alpine Way road in the Snowy Mountains and it goes up and down steeply. This is quite a lot of work for our car brakes. They start to burn and smell badly, yelling, "Gimme a break, man!" And we do. Quite frequently. Snow covers gum trees by the roadside but the road is nice and dry. The Alpine National Park gradually becomes the Snowy Mountains, and then Kosciuszko National Park near a town called Khancoban. The highest official peak lies somewhere in the vicinity. Whether this is the highest point of Australia as such is debatable, because there are three substantially higher peaks on Australian external territories, Mount McClintock and Mount Menzies in Antarctica, and Mawson Peak on the small islands of Heard and McDonald. But they are far, far away and Mount Kosciuszko can enjoy a sweet monopoly. Some people might laugh at its height, but come here in winter and walk it up in snow. These are our thoughts in Jindabyne, where having replenished supplies, we're set for the mountains.

57
Why Mount Kosciuszko

The initial plan was to rent skis—standard cross-country ones—and avoid the chairlift at all cost, because that's for sissies. Then get to the place called Dead Horse Gap and walk up the ten kilometres or so, and ideally, back. The first snag: the information ladies don't want to tell much beyond the official touristy claptrap. "Are you very, very, very experienced?" one of them asks us with a stern look, as if we had asked for something illegal.

We buy a topographic map. The ski rental announces that normal cross-country skis are out of the goddamn question, they're not renting them to us under any circumstances. We need sturdier back-country skis. They don't want to have anything to do with our broken limbs.

"It's this or nothing," a Swiss guy in the ski rental says. "You need to buy a compass. We're not renting it."

"We're only going straight up and then straight down," I try to be funny but sound stupid.

"Yeah, yeah, look, I'll at least show you where to go," he replies.

Ngariro Campground is within the national park border. We drive there for the night so that we can start very early the next day. Ice patches cover the tent canvas in the morning.

The track up to Mount Kosciuszko from Dead Horse Gap is not overzealously marked. There are high snow poles, but otherwise it's down to the map and common sense. Most people just want to go to the peak by chairlift, walk the remaining distance on foot and tick off the highest mountain of the continent. Thredbo is their refuge. It's excellent for seasonal daddies with kids chained to their legs but a bit boring for somebody who wants to get a better picture of the area, especially when you want to create conditions closer to those of the early explorers. Those who want lower prices go to Jindabyne. Forewarned is forearmed. We can do without Thredbo.

On the way up the highest mountain

The morning is very foggy and there's barely any light. We put our shoes on, and the skis, pack some warm clothes in the backpack because the temperature is minus one degree Celsius. We take lots of water, food, and the industrial gloves we used for corn castration in Kununurra. They are greenish in colour but will do the job. Two crucial items are left behind in the car, but we don't know it yet.

The ascent is steep at first, and so it's more about marching up rather than skiing. We need to get higher onto the mountain ridge and then pull through a thick eucalyptus forest. After about an hour, the trail becomes slightly less demanding, with trees thinning out and shrubs and smaller gum trees appearing. Here and there larger rocks emerge, and we follow the ski path made by more adventurous people before us.

Final ascent to Mount Kosciuszko, NSW

The fog is almost gone, visibility improves but the sky is still nowhere in sight. Metabolism has kicked in and the cold feeling from the morning is gone. After about two hours, we can see the first skiers from the Thredbo village. A wide open snowy plain is ahead, with occasional information signs partly or entirely covered in snow. The sun peeks briefly from behind the curtain, but quickly pops back and stays put. Another hour and we're at the foot of the mountain; at least that's what we think, from a broken cluster of planks pretending to be a signpost. Mount Kosciuszko is not immediately recognisable. It even seems to be lower than the surrounding peaks, especially the one next to it—Mount Townsend, named after Thomas Townsend, the guy who later became First Viscount Sydney (and couldn't help but leave his name behind in the largest city). Everything is under snow and so we take to the shortest path uphill, which points left. It's a slow ascent that takes at least an hour, and all of a sudden the sun crawls from under the cloud and decides to stay. After locating a ski track again, the ascent becomes easier. We're almost at the top.

In 1839 Sir Paul Edmund Strzelecki[63] came here with two English companions, James Riley and James McArthur, and two Aboriginal guides "Charlie" and "Jackie". They were here to map the highest point of the land.

"There we are gents, the highest peak of New Holland!"

"New South Wales," somebody corrects.

"No, of the lot I think—" Sir Edmund insists.

"Shall we say something for the record?" says one of them to lift the mood.

Thirty seconds of silence.

All look around, then back at one another.

"Won't go any higher, will it, Jackie? You reckon?"

"No" says the Aboriginal guide.

Silence.

"Soooo, it's this one over there, is it?" Riley starts again.

"Naaa, the one on the left," replies McArthur.

"Charlie?"

"Yeah, it's that one."

Silence again.

"Well, not much to look at is it?" McArthur says finally, with a

---

63 Strzelecki Memorial in Jindabyne, NSW https://goo.gl/maps/H4hEpByDZVn

VIII. Melbourne to Sydney

frown.

"What are we puttin' it down as?" Riley again.

Now all turning their eyes into the map and then back on the mountain.

"It looks like a bloody tomb I saw back home in Krakow," says Strzelecki.

General chuckling.

"What was the name of it? Riley asks.

"Yeah, sure! Gipps will be over the moon about this. He can't even say *my* name."

He packs his stuff back in his rucksack and is quiet for a moment.

"Do you know what's long and hard that a bride gets when she marries a Polish guy?" Sir Edmund continues.

Nobody has a clue.

"Her new last name."

Mount Kosciuszko[64], 2,228 m ASL

---

64 Mount Kosciuszko, NSW https://goo.gl/maps/7MiPSN4XEFA2

*

The sun is at its best now. We foolishly enjoy it, not realising that in the evening we're going to bitterly regret it. We didn't bother taking sun cream and glasses because the weather was so hopelessly bad in the morning. A silly mistake.

There is a handful of people at the top, their skis stuck deep in snow and all having a warm cuppa. There's nothing better than hot tea but soon time is up. The descent is steep at first, then it evens out, but the path that brought us here has disappeared. It all looks different now. Knowing that down there somewhere must be a river, we can't go too far wrong and we enter the thick forest, legs waist-deep in snow, cold half-frozen gloves and brutally, brutally burned faces.

*

It starts with a warm heat all around the head in the evening. By night there are water blisters around the cheeks, and by morning the skin is stinging and hurts badly, all over our faces. Our eyes are constantly teary, red and sore. We can't sleep and our vision is blurred. Snow blindness. We somehow get to Jindabyne and spend the whole next day there to pull ourselves together.

Driving on the following day is very difficult. We stop to pick up a suicidal turtle lying in the middle of the road. No, it's not that bad. We can hear it speak, "Leave me alone, people, I am safe in my shell."

The landscape is changing now. What was lush and green becomes monotonously brown and yellow. The mountains on the other side of the Great Dividing Range don't get as much water. And so yellow goes on and on.

Yellow: that's the presage of Canberra.

58
Canberra in a Nutshell

To make up for the yellow monotony that Canberra is surrounded with from each direction, the capital organises an annual flower festival called Floriade. Flowers are everywhere, of all kinds and all shapes. The more colours the better.

Canberra is a town made with one thing in mind: to represent. Beautiful for some, ugly for others, it's spread out like a middle-aged chubby wife on a public beach, knowing that guys will notice but not touch. A bit like a marvel of technology, designed on a board, man-made, thought through, fairly inventive. The large roundabouts visible from the Parliament Hill pour out into long and wide parallel streets. The "layout" is probably best enjoyed from the TV tower. The city was designed for a million people or so but only about one third of that number live there, enough prominents for the prices to keep up with Sydney and Melbourne—mainly government small- and bigwigs. One of our friends told us once that if we stumble on it sometime, and can't find anywhere to sleep, we can try to take a few pictures of the American or Israeli embassies. They would take care of us no time. But he didn't mention the price so we're heading on. We're not into cities. We're out of them.

59
Mountains Upside Down

If we were inmates of an average Australian prison somewhere out there, "Goulburn" would send shivers down our spines and we'd be told its name each time somebody wanted to put us back in line. Goulburn has reputation for being one of the toughest prisons in the country, hosting all kinds of the most fearsome criminal elements, the most notorious names. It stands on a hill and it would have a nice view over the town, if the guys had windows.

Other than that, it's just a town and the home of the Big Merino. She stands there by the road as a symbol of a once profitable industry. The wool business has been sabotaged by fake cheap synthetics and it has fallen out of grace. We can buy the good stuff here, and even see how it was made.

Big Merino, Goulburn, NSW

Australia has something in the vicinity of ninety million sheep. About seventy-five per cent are merinos, the rest are crossbred. The merino was imported from Spain and has been around for as long as anyone here can remember—that is, the end of the eighteenth century. The breed has toughened up in incredibly harsh conditions to become probably the most resilient home animal of all time.

*

We were given an address, "Turn left to Kialla, follow the dirt road until you find an old large fridge. That's our mailbox. Then follow the road uphill until you reach our house."

Keith looks a bit like George Bush. He lives in an old farmhouse and has lots of cows that chew on anything they can find during the hot day: the yellow grass that dominates the local countryside and silage he throws from his tractor every evening.

"I had a mowing business in Sydney a while ago, but I bailed out. The city is not for me any more." He lives with his girlfriend who still works in Sydney—now only about two hours away. He lights up a cigarette and looks like everybody can just kiss his arse. Nothing will knock him off. He owns the whole forest nearby. It's going to be his retirement when the time arrives.

Mountains inverted: Wollemi, NSW

Kanangra Boyd is the closest national park on the way north. On the map it's the incredibly vast green patch south west of Sydney. It's got a karst area called Jenolan Caves. Good for a stop. There is another and even a bigger green patch about two hours north called Wollemi National Park. Most Australians on hearing that name will say something like: "Oh yeah, that's where they found the prehistoric tree." That's right. The Wollemi Pine was found by pure chance in 1994 when a hiker ventured into the most remote parts of the park and got into an isolated gorge, set off from the rest of the bush. "Nice tree," he thought. Nothing like anything else. He brought home a sample. *Wollemia nobilis* has survived since Jurassic time, which was about two hundred million years ago. They say there are only about hundred of them in the wild and only a small circle of insiders know where the place is: a public secret. One day this planet might be without people again, but the nobilis could still be alive. Unbelievable when you translate it into distance. If the tree had travelled two hundred kilometres, the whole known history of humankind would have only got somewhere within the boundary of fifty metres.

Oil shell refinery ruins in Newnes

The entire area of the Wollemi National Park are inverted mountains. In Europe, people settled in the valleys first and then went up as far as the conditions allowed. Here, it's the other way round and so when you hike, you leave civilisation going down first and then climb back to it. But the mountains are so vast that often you need to drive down, not hike, then drive back up. Like Newnes, for instance, where the ruins of an oil-shell factory are hidden deep in the woods. It was still in full swing at the beginning of the twentieth century.

Oil-shell rock was destructed and extracts distilled from it were pumped up the hill for further processing. The foundations are now covered by moss and grass and are gradually being claimed back by nature to become one again. There is also a large and free camp surrounded by high rock walls. Also a discontinued long and dark train tunnel where glow-worms now live. It's a great walk in complete darkness with hundreds of miniature lights around.

VIII. Melbourne to Sydney

Glow Worm Tunnel[65]

Tomorrow we're going west again for one last time. Because there is a place in New South Wales like no other: Hill End.

---

65 Glow worm tunnel near Newnes, NSW https://goo.gl/maps/MVtoXzPdrJS2

IX. Golden Epilogue

60
Where Freedom Begins: Hill End

Just as Western Australia has had its pearling frenzy and South Australia has had its opal glory, Victoria and New South Wales have had their gold rushes.

Remarkably, in a matter of only few years whole villages and towns were born and only a few year later after gold was gone, they all but disappeared. We're going to Hill End which in 1873 was the second largest town in New South Wales. History is the town and the town is the history.

Today it's just a dot on a map with nothing around it but hills, and it feels like the end of the world. There are only three roads to get there: The first one from Mudgee, second one from Bathurst, through another gold-digging hub called Sofala, and the third and roughest one from Bathurst through hills called Bridle Track[66]. It used to be a horse trail.

Our hatchback does quite well on the 4WD-only track, but the truth is, it's not so comfortable. The road goes uphill along quite a steep rock face, and occasionally it closes due to falling rocks. A huge boulder fell on it, about halfway along, at a place called Monaghan's Bluff. The local council feels too insignificant to fix the problem and the state government—for change—feels too important to bother about rural roads. We are lucky the boulder has chosen another time. We'd be as flat as the road it rested its enormous weight upon.

The Bridle Track goes up and down until it reaches a causeway through Turon River. We're rather tired by then. The weather is hot again as we move north and change altitude, and the river offers

---
66 Bridle Track near Hill End, NSW https://goo.gl/maps/NuZeGsDPMgm

plenty of shade. We're just about to jump in it when an old 4x4 arrives. From Bathurst we passed no more than two or three cars, but none of them driven by a hippie woman with four dogs sitting by her side. She pulls down her window.

"Do we know you?" she asks in a bored voice. "We," means "she and her goodly German shepherds".

"Oh, hi, I don't think so," I say unconvincingly.

The dogs now start to bark loudly.

"Well. Who cares! Let's have a swim," and she slowly drives through the causeway to the other bank. Before we know it, she takes off her clothes and she and the dogs all splash in the water. She has an enormous tattoo immediately above her mons.

Remote hills between Bathurst and Hill End, NSW

After driving up the last bit from the river to the town, we find ourselves in the second half of the nineteenth century. New South Wales was just about to end the penal transports, and as conditions started to improve for ordinary people, was opened for immigration, and not only from Britain—far from it. The immigrants were typically poor and the new country didn't enjoy a good reputation. It didn't have an official name and was regarded second-category, where people went out of desperation rather than choice. And their motivation grew with the knowledge that this new world provided rare new opportunities.

Gold was first catalogued officially by Dmitri Mendeleev in his periodic table in 1869, but people knew it for thousands of years. It's about the only material that can withstand whims of time and so be used as universal store of value. Especially in bad times like these, what could be better than an opportunity to dig some out, then sell it and reach for economic independence? And that's what drove most people in here. Gold was their ticket to freedom.

The smallest continent might be infantile in political terms, but in regards to geology it's the oldest grandma in town. A few hundred million years ago, the earth's plates moved and caused huge eruptions, which then hurled a large numbers of liquid rocks called quartz to its surface. With quartz, they also released "dirt". After the eruptions cooled down, the rock then hardened and the small particles got into rivers, more precisely into their lowest layers, because gold is heavier than anything around it.

The first mentions of gold are said to have come from Portuguese maps. They tagged the north-western coast of Australia as Costa d'Ouro. Nobody knows why, but this continent was associated with gold from the very beginnings. If Cook dug a few hundred metres under his flag in Queensland, he'd have found a field with two and a half thousand ounces of gold.

Publishing this kind of information however was taboo for a long time. As early as 1823, a certain James McBrien stumbled across gold when exploring rivers, then Edmund Strzelecki did the same during his geological studies, and so did William Branwhite Clarke, around 1841. The governor of the time, Sir George Gipps, made it blatantly clear to them to keep their mouths shut, because he knew what kind of ragtag flock lived in the colonies.

The information was spread only after making sure there was enough gold to make livelihoods for many people and for many years.

The New South Wales mountains were impenetrable for a long

time, and settlement started much later than on the coast. Bathurst was the first significant town outside Sydney that was founded inland, and had a certain peculiarity. The river flew west and not east to the sea, as would normally be expected. The first settlers thought that it might end in an unknown lake, and around 1815 they started to search for it. This was one of the reasons the Bridle Track was formed between Bathurst and another town called Wellington, to the west. It was later used for moving cattle herds, but Bridle Track was there long "before" gold.

Then three gentlemen, Edward Hammond Hargraves, John Lister and James Tom, discovered in 1851 the first significant gold deposit in a place called Yorkies Creek, twenty-nine kilometres north east of Orange. Only then did the authorities realise that it could actually benefit the local land, and immigration was justified. Hargraves was rewarded and appointed Commissioner of Crown Lands, and while indulging in large quantities of rum—then the most valuable article in the colony—he had Yorkies Creek renamed for the biblical Ophir. He forgot his mates and let the new discovery be associated with his name only.

A short time later, gold was discovered in Dirt Holes Creek, near Tambaroora on the Turon River[67] on about a twenty-five kilometre stretch with Hill End in its middle. The following twenty years were a gold rush of unimaginable proportions and an incredible boost for the local economy. By claiming only a little chunk of those new riches, one could get a shortcut to the higher society.

61
It's Panning Out

We're going on a gold-panning tour with a guide who is going to show us what the business is about. We're to wait near the "red chimneys", which are the ruins of one of the local houses in a de facto ghost town called Tambaroora —the one before Hill End. Houses used to have chimneys and the solitary chimneys were

---

67 Turon River, NSW https://goo.gl/maps/ML9MnvoMK6n

usually what were left of the buildings long after people left and their houses fell apart. There are hardly any houses standing now. There is one spooky cemetery and everywhere around, there are deep cavities as scars of the time, giving away the town's past.

Fred—who looks like the front page of a Lonely Planet guide—arrives in an old red Falcon, in dirty old leather hat. His wrinkly face is "cleanly unshaven", he has a slow oscillating pace and is about seventy-five and pretty fit. In five minutes we're driving on a narrow dirt road to check the creek where he knows good spots. He gets out of his car, grabs his shovel and immediately begins to work. He digs deep in the river, scoops some debris into his black gold pan, separates the larger pieces with his gloves, throws stones and dirt away, then, with a fast flick of his hand takes the upper layer away and sloshes the rest in water. He then repeats the cycle a few more times until only a small amount of dirt stays in the pan. He keeps sloshing the remaining mud until only a spoonful of water resides on its bottom and somehow he separates only a few small dust particles, so that they stay on one side of the pan, not even a centimetre apart, while the rest of the worthless dirt goes back in the creek. After that he licks his index finger, touches the dust gently, takes out a small water-filled ampoule, presses the finger on it, and shakes it gently. Finally, he seals it off with a plug.

"There you go. Gold." He says.

He does a few more rounds, then sits down. He lights up a cigarette, and comfortably leaning against a stump he continues.

"Gold is still in the river here but very little. After a hundred and fifty years, you know, not much is left. The trick is to get to the very bottom of the creek, through to the thickest mud layer where gold can't drop any further. It won't get under the clay. Then you just take it."

It looks easy. I try to imitate him but I fail badly. My panning is slow and clumsy. Water in the pan is desperately dancing all over it, it splashes from side to side, as if saying to me in frustration, "What the hell do you want me to do? Make up your mind!" In the first few dishes I can't see anything at all.

Meanwhile, Fred sits nearby, smokes and watches. It takes me at least one century to finish one dish. My back hurts more after each one.

"Twenty-eight seconds one dish," he squeezes suddenly through his ciggy.

"Yeah, not me. I couldn't live on it," I admit. "How do you do it?"

"Years and years, mate."

I give up. There is no difference between mastering gold panning and the piano. Both require years of practising. Fred is a virtuoso.

There were a few categories of gold-diggers. Thousands of losers who sacrificed their health and life, never actually getting anywhere. There were those who found it, got rich, but no matter what they did after, we don't know anything about them. And last, there were those who made it, thrived, and documented everything for us. One of those was Bernard Holtermann.

62
In Which Otto Won his Lotto

Bernhardt Otto Holtermann, a German immigrant from Hamburg, was a success story, a textbook example of what a person can achieve in the new world with a bit of luck and a lot of hard work.

He arrived around 1855 when he was twenty. He did whatever he could with his limited English: a jackaroo, photo shop assistant, and a waiter in a Sydney hotel named after his hometown. It was a well-known gold-digging hub and it seemed—the place to be. That's where he met Hugo Luis Beyers, a native of Posen, who already knew a thing or two about Tambaroora. It was right next to Hill End, where the German Town quarter was.

Beyers and Holtermann got a prospecting claim on a land lot in

Hill End. Their joint venture was called Star of Hope. They did it in their spare time because they had to sustain themselves with other work. They looked after a hotel.

Hill End, NSW: 1873 versus present time

Life in Hill End wasn't easy. There were many who arrived only to scuttle back to Sydney before even buying a pickaxe. The conditions were so harsh. Holtermann himself nearly lost his life when an explosion went off, almost burying him alive. It was a time of the second gold rush, when most gold lumps had already been extracted and what they now had to work with was alluvial gold in nuggets, found together with quartz. It was hard, debilitating work in which heavy specimens had to be pulled out of the ground for further processing. To finance operations, Beyers and Holtermann sold smaller shares to six other people, thus creating a syndicate. They did okay, but no breakthrough came until 12 October 1872, towards the very end of the gold rush. They pulled out a specimen of gold and quartz, the largest of its kind ever found. The lot weighed about three hundred kilograms, the gold yield was said to be about eighty-five kilos. They quit and started to do business. Beyers was later conned by a friend who had looked after his estate and eventually went broke, returning to mining.

Holtermann was more successful: he imported goods from Germany, made and sold medicinal drops, entered politics and pursued his passion—photography, in those days a totally new and expensive discipline. He commissioned an extensive photo project with photographers Beaufoy and Merlin, capturing the life of ordinary people in the colonies. They successfully exhibited in Europe and America. After realising the power of pictures, he used a photo composition of himself with the golden nugget to market his products.

Otto Bernard Holtermann

Interestingly enough, in those times of real economy, when *owning* was not confused with *owing*, he did not call himself a millionaire. Yet he built a few-storey, multi-room stone mansion with an elevated tower, overlooking Sydney Harbour, now unfortunately not accessible to public because it's owned by a posh Anglican private school establishment called Shore. Had he counted his blessings in today's inflated economy, his share of gold would have roughly got him a habitable, mediocre, four-bedroom fibro house in an average Sydney suburb. Times have changed. At some later point in history, Mr Governments had a wild binge with Ms Banks, and together they sent their former boss, Mr Gold, packing. Today, they teach everybody to count in six figures without the need to have any tangible wealth. And so, who said gold could not be manufactured after all? Dirty sweated-in overalls went out of fashion. It's more about shiny Versace suits now.

Anyway, as a member of parliament for St Leonards in 1883, Holtermann also apparently came up with a bold idea, "... *tzz* bridge *von* Milson's Point to Sydney? How'z that?" The nobility of the time just rolled their eyes and couldn't see the point. The Sydney Harbour Bridge saw the light of day in 1932. Some say at the very same coordinates he had envisioned fifty years earlier.

Just as he had about everything he ever wanted, he died of cancer at only forty-seven years old. Holtermann's gold-digging success, however, was just a prelude to something much bigger. One hundred years later, in the 1950s, somebody searched an old shed and miraculously stumbled across three thousand perfectly preserved, extremely fragile glass plate negatives documenting, in the most vivid detail, the lives of the settlers in those times.

They are worth more than gold now[68].

63
Big Smoke

After two hours of teaching us how to get the remaining gold out of the creek, Fred only asks a few miserable dollars. We can't believe he's doing this almost for free. "Now bloody Centrelink makes sure you don't get rich. If you earn too much, they'll cut payments. My friend Rick earned a few bucks on the side and reported it. He's not doing it anymore. You have to like what you're doing. Every year I swear I'm done with it. But I still do it."

"I know people came here on school excursions," I say to him.

"Yeah, they've been coming for years. Kids from Sydney who only know concrete. Not like country kids. A Filipino girl asked me recently if I could lick her finger to scoop the gold dust from the pan, because the water was too dirty for her. Or there was a brat who threw my tools in the river. I had to search for them in the mud, waist-deep in water. And then he dobbed me in to his

---

[68] Holtermann Collection at State Library, NSW: http://www2.sl.nsw.gov.au/archive/discover_collections/society_art/photography/holtermann/

IX. Golden Epilogue

teacher when I sent him to the bus. Huuuge difference between city kids and country kids."

"So you're retired now?"

"Yeah but I am still doing things. I've been digging graves too. Now there's only two funerals a year. Terrible. It used to be much better."

The tip of the Holtermann's nugget is in the local private museum. The owner of History Hill,[69] with his beard down his belly button, shows us around his amazing lifetime creation. Ten thousand artefacts.

"I offered students free food and accommodation in exchange for archiving it. Not interested."

There is everything here; a replica of a long ventilation shaft, a geology expo, many tools of the period, spare parts, all kinds of containers, detailed description of trades of the time, old pictures, boxes, clothes, shoes, books, notes, even complete large machines that used to crush earth at day and night. Hill End used to be a noisy town. When the machines broke down, people couldn't sleep because the silence was so deafening.

We're sitting in the pub in the evening, the only one that has survived out of thirty others gone with the wind. A family of wallabies are grazing in sun that's going to sink in a few minutes. They chew grass slowly. Squeaking sounds of birds can be heard from the trees behind them.

Where has everybody gone? Time really does seem to pass much more slowly after three months of no distractions, flat screens, boring commercials, internet, e-mail, socials, dates, meetings, every-day routine; it's spiritually renewing. It has a calming effect on both body and mind. If only for that one thing, it is definitely worth the effort. The main discovery.

Everything is merging as if it had started yesterday, but I've lost exact count of the days. Maybe I should write it all down.

69 History Hill, Hill End, NSW https://goo.gl/maps/J8Q23rEUhFU2

63 Big Smoke

And maybe I should forget all about it.

A few kilometres from here and we're on the threshold of Sydney again, the jovial, semi-pompous urban hub, where, because of the climate, you never know for sure if you're still on holidays weeks after coming back to work, but where stress can catch up with you just like any other place of similar size in the world. It forms from western, yellowish plains, gradually building into a conglomerate of patched land blobs that quickly make room for the ever-growing concrete suburbia, where houses stand in an orderly fashion, one next to another, and their small yards are neatly separated by high metal fences. Many fences.

And right behind all that is the shiny city that shows off its glamorous venues and tempts tourists with its icons, passing itself off as the real, true, indispensable image of the country. That's also Australia. But it's another story.

APPENDIX

Glossary

ABN – Australian Business Number

ANZAC – Australian and New Zealand Army Corps

ASL – above sea level

APC – Arms, Pits and Crotch; quick wash

Abo – a pejorative short for Aboriginal

billabong – a stagnant pool of water; dead-end of a stream or river

big smoke – any large city in Australia (originally Aboriginal description)

bindy, pl. bindies – sharp thorn, thorns in grass

bloke – slang for a male

bludger – a good-for-nothing; a lazy person

boab tree – an Australian tree unique to the Kimberley region; it has a thick trunk often in a shape of a bottle; 'bottle' tree

bogan – not very sophisticated, unrefined person; a chav (UK)

brownish – brown or similar (similarly gold*ish* – gold and similar, etc.)

CBD – City Business District

Centrelink – Australian welfare offices

chock-a-block – fully occupied; busy

croc – a crocodile

damper – simple Australian bread popular with swagmen

didgeridoo – a wind instrument of indigenous Australians

dirt road – gravel road

dodgy – something of questionable quality

dough – money; cash

dugout – a house or other underground property

dunny, pl. dunnies – slang for a toilet, bog

duty of care – a moral or legal obligation to ensure the safety or well-being of others

fair enough – used to admit that something is reasonable or acceptable; okay, I agree

far out – cool

Freo – a nickname for Fremantle (a town in Western Australia)

freshie – a freshwater crocodile

fruitcake – an eccentric mad person; a nutter

goodie – a good or favoured character

goon – cheap Australian wine bought in a cardboard box

hatch – a short for hatchback car

humpy – a small, temporary shelter made from bark and tree branches, traditionally used by Australian Aboriginals

inselberg – an island mountain

jackaroo – a young man working on a sheep or cattle station

legend – a person revered for something; often *fucking legend* to describe somebody who is absolutely cool or excessively proud or complacent

lilo – to ride an inflatable mattress on a running stream of water

morning tea – a small meal or snack eaten between breakfast and lunch

mozzies – mosquitoes

nanny state – an overprotective system that tries to prevent everything before it happens

noodling – rummaging in piles of dirt and rubble to find opal

NSW – New South Wales

NT – Northern Territory

odo – odometer

Pollywaffle – Australian chocolate bar brand; a popular name to describe a piece of shit because it's brown and it's about the same size

potch – opal without much colour or worth

Powerball – a successful Australian lottery game modelled on its American namesake

PR – permanent residency

Qantas – Australian flag carrier company; the largest Australian airline

QLD – Queensland

redback – a small venomous spider

relly, pl. rellies – relative, relatives

roo – a short for kangaroo

saltie – a saltwater crocodile

SA – South Australia

Skip – an Anglo-Saxon Australian, a synonym for a "fair dinkum" Aussie, derived from the Australian TV show 'Skippy' starring a Kangaroo from the Australian bushland

spinifex – sharp-pointed Australian grass

spud – a potato

strewth – an exclamation used to express surprise or dismay, short for "God's truth"

sheila – slang for a female

Telstra – a big telecom company often known for its recalcitrant attitude

thongs – light sandals with a thong between the big end second toe, slippers, jandals (NZ), flip-flops (UK)

Trabi – Trabbi, pl. Trabbies, Trabant, a two-stroke engine East German car with plastic upper body, notorious for breakdowns

tradie, pl. tradies – a tradesman, tradesmen

tucker – Australian slang for food

VIC – Victoria

WA – Western Australia

whinger – a constantly complaining person

Map

Noteworthy Mountaints and Peaks

Mount McClintock; 3,490 m ASL, the Australian Antarctic Territory

Mount Menzies; 3,355 m ASL, the Australian Antarctic Territory

Mawson Peak; 2,745 m ASL, the Heard and McDonald Islands

Mount Kosciuszko; 2,228 m ASL, Snowy Mountains, NSW

Mount Townsend; 2,209 m ASL, Snowy Mountains, NSW

Mount Sonder / Rwetyepme; 1.380 m ASL, West MacDonnell Ranges, NT

Mount Meharry / Wirlbiwirlbi; 1245 m ASL, Karijini National Park, WA

Mount Bruce / Punurrunha; 1,234 m ASL, Karijini National Park, WA

St Mary Peak / Ngarri Mudlanha; 1,171 m ASL, Ikara-Flinders Ranges, SA

Mount Nameless / Jarndunmunha; 1,128 m ASL, Karijini National Park, WA

Mount Conner / Atilla; 859 m ASL, near Uluru, NT

Mount Stapylton, Grampians / Gariwerd; 244 m ASL, VIC

Hollow Mountain, Grampians / Gariwerd; around 240 ASL, VIC

Mount Arapiles / Djurite; around 140 m ASL, VIC

Route and Refuelling

Day | From | To (km) | Total (km) | Full tank (X) | Spare fuel jerry can (x)

1 | Perth - Balcatta | 33 | 33 | X

2 | Perth Balcatta - Pinnacles | 287 | 320

Pinnacles - Jurien Bay | 49 | 369 | X

3 | Jurien Bay - Geraldton | 207 | 576 | X

Geraldton - Neren Neren | 184 | 760

4 | Neren Neren - Overlander Roadhouse | 94 | 854

Overlander Roadhouse - Carnarvon | 210 | 1064 | Xx

5 | Carnarvon - Exmouth/Lighthouse Carpark | 281 | 1354

6 | Exmouth - Cape Range National Park | 152 | 1497 | X

7 | Exmouth   Nanutarra Roadhouse | 210 | 1707

Nanutarra Roadhouse - Paraburdoo | 369 | 2076 | X

Paraburdoo - Tom Price | 80 | 2156

8 | Tom Price - Karijini NP/Savannah | 109 | 2265 | X

9 | Karijini NP/Savannah - Karijini/Dales | 55 | 2320

10 | Karijini NP/Dales - Mt. Bruce | 194 | 2514

11 | Karijini NP/Dales - Auski Roadhouse | 83 | 2597

Auski Roadhouse - South Hedland | 262 | 2859 | X

12 | Port Hedland - Sandfire Roadhouse | 216 | 3075 | Xx

13 | Sandfire Roadhouse - Broome/Roebuck | 290 | 3365

Broome/Roebuck - Broome | 58 | 3423 | Xx

14 | Broome - Willare Bridge Roadhouse | 166 | 3589

Willare Bridge Roadhouse - Fitzroy Crossing | 245 | 3834 | X

15 | Fitzroy C'/Geiki Gorge NP - Halls Creek | 350 | 4184 | X

Halls Creek (China Wall) - Spring Creek | 70 | 4254 | X

16 | Spring Creek Rest Area - Turkey Creek | 187 | 4441

APPENDIX

Turkey Creek - Wyndham/Crocodile Farm | 100 | 4541

Wyndham - King River Restplace | 63 | 4604 | X

17 | King River Restplace - Kununurra | 116 | 4720

18 | Kununurra

19 | Kununurra

20 | Kununurra

21 | Kununurra

22 | Kununurra - Lake Argyle Tourist Village | 114 | 4834

23 | Lake Argyle Tourist Village - NT Border | 48 | 4882 | X

24 | NT Border - "62 Mile Restplace"/Victoria River | 413 | 5295

"62 Mile Restplace"/Victoria River - Katherine | 110 | 5405 | X

25 | Katherine - Nitmiluk NP/Katherine Gorge | 100 | 5505 | X

26 | Katherine - Edith Falls/Nitmiluk NPark | 60 | 5565

Edith Falls - Douglas Hot Springs NP | 192 | 5757

27 | Douglas Hot Springs NP - Bachelor | 130 | 5887

Bachelor - Litchfield National Park | 49 | 5936

28 | Litchfield National Park - Darwin | 362 | 6298 | X

Darwin - Darwin | 161 | 6459 | X

29 | Darwin - Jabiru/Kakadu NP | 369 | 6828

30 | Jabiru/Kakadu NP - Nourlangie Walk | 70 | 6898 | X

Nourlangie - Yellow Waters | 39 | 6937

31 | Yellow Waters - Katherine | 261 | 7198

Katherine - Mataranka /Elsey NP | 120 | 7318 | X

32 | Mataranka/Elsey National Park - Elliot | 329 | 7647

Elliot - Marry Ann /Tennant Creek | 255 | 7902 | X

33 | Marry Ann /Wauchope - Alice Springs/Wintersun | 533 | 8435 | X

34 | Alice Springs - Alice Springs | 30 | 8465 | Xx

35 | Alice Springs - Ormiston Gorge | 173 | 8638

36 | Ormiston Gorge - Mt. Sonder | 57 | 8695

37 | Glen Helen - Alice Springs | 159 | 8854

38 | Alice Springs - Erldunda | 112 | 8966 | X

39 | Erldunda - Curtin Springs | 148 | 9114

Curtin Springs - Yulara | 176 | 9290 | X

40| "Restplace" Yulara - Uluru/Ayers Rock | 30 | 9320

Uluru/Ayers Rock - Kata Tjuta/Olgas | 55 | 9375

Kata Tjuta/Olgas - Uluru/Ayers Rock | 55 | 9430

Uluru/Yulara - Curtin Springs | 89 | 9519 | X

41 | Curtin Springs - Kings Canyon | 228 | 9747

Kings Canyon - Mt. Ebenezer Roadhouse | 113 | 9860

42 | Mt. Ebenezer Roadhouse - Kulgera | 13 | 9873 | X

Kulgera - Marla | 183 | 10056

Marla - Cadney Roadhouse | 80 | 10136 | X

43 | Cadney Roadhouse - Breakaways | 160 | 10296

Breakaways - Coober Pedy | 30 | 10326

44 | Coober Pedy - Coober Pedy | 20 | 10346 | X

45 | Coober Pedy - Bon Bon Rest Area | 191 | 10537

46 | Bon Bon Rest Area - Woomera | 121 | 10658

Pimba - Hawker | 283 | 10941 | X

47 | Hawker - Flinders Ranges NP/Wilpena Pound | 137 | 11078

48 | Flinders Ranges NP/St Mary Peak

49 | Wilpena Pound - Quorn | 125 | 11203

50 | Quorn - Port Augusta | 156 | 11359 | X

51 | Port Augusta - Adelaide | 253 | 11612 | X

52 | Adelaide - Adelaide | 10 | 11622

53 | Adelaide - Murray Bridge | 80 | 11702

Murray Bridge - Naracoorte | 305 | 12007 | X

54 | Naracoorte

55 | Naracoorte - Mt Arapiles | 199 12206 | X

56 | Mt Arapiles - Stawell | 170 | 12376

57 | Stawell - Grampians NP/Wonderland | 90 | 12466

58 | Stawell - Grampians NP/Mt Stapylton | 116 | 12582 | X

59 | Stawell - Warrnambool | 308 | 12890

60 | Warrnambool | X

61 | Warrnambool - Lorne/Cumberland Carpark | 271 | 13161

62 | Lorne - Torquay | 76 | 13237

63 | Torquay - Melbourne | 120 | 13357 | X

64 | Melbourne

65 | Melbourne

66 | Melbourne

67 | Melbourne - Melbourne | 349 | 13706

68 | Melbourne - Benalla | 248 | 13954 | X

69 | Benalla - Bright/Mt Buffalo NP | 106 | 14060

70 | Bright - Corryong | 206 | 14266

71 | Corryong - Jindabyne | 120 | 14386 | X

72 | Jindabyne - Kosciuszko NP/Ngarigo | 36 | 14422

Kosciuszko NP/Dead Horse Gap - Jindabyne | 100 | 14522

73 | Jindabyne/Caravan Park - Canberra | 218 | 14740

74 | Canberra - Canberra | 50 | 14790 | X

75 | Canberra - Goulburn/Kialla | 192 | 14982 | X

76 | Kialla - Oberon | 159 | 15141

77 | Oberon - Jenolan Caves | 74 | 15215

78 | Jenolan Caves - Leura/Blue Mountains NP | 81 | 15296 | X

79 | Leura - Lithgow | 165 | 15461

80 | Lithgow - Newnes/Wollemi NP | 48 | 15509

81 | Newnes - Bathurst | 84 | 15593

82 | Bathurst - Hill End | 75 | 15668

83 | Hill End - Hill End | 117 | 15785 | X
84 | Hill End - Bathurst | 75 | 15860
Bathurst - Sydney | 201 | 16061 | X

Travel Budget Hints

ITEM: % of budget

Petrol: 23.3 % (A); refuelling 46 times

Food: 23.4 % (B);

Equipment: 11.1 % (C)

Car maintenance, registration, penalties: 15.4 % (D)

Accommodation: 10.8 % (E)

National park fees: 2.75 % (F)

Miscellaneous: 13.25 % (G)

Based on this information you can easily calculate the very minimum cost of a budget travel through the continent, e. g.:

Assuming consumption of 9 litres of petrol per 100 km: 46 refuellings *times* the size of your petrol/diesel tank *times* current price of 1 litre petrol/diesel = A

At the time of our journey an average bread roll cost twice the price of one litre of petrol. If price of petrol or diesel shoots up, the food share on the total budget will have to be adjusted accordingly. This way you can calculate "B".

We don't live of bread only but this will do as a very rough estimate. The ratio of the two items tells a lot about the current price level and works surprisingly well.

C, D, E, F, and G can then be extrapolated from the percentages.

Not to forget

A first-aid kit in a car is not compulsory in Australia, but it should be the first thing any sensible and serious traveller buys. They often sell them with survival and emergency handbooks. Carry both of those items with you all the time

A good torch can be handy in many situations. Carry most of the times

2 sets of thongs: showers in the outback are often dirty

Personal hygiene

Basic medicine

Suncream: lots and lots of it

Sun glasses: buy more and have them always within arm's reach

Water container: it needs to be kept full all the time

Fuel container: it might not be necessary but it can be helpful

Pencil tyre gauge

Dust pan and brush

Battery charger, jump start kit

Spray cleaner

Kitchen utensils, travel dishes, fry pan

Good sleeping bags and pillows

Good mattresses

Tent

Gas burner and fuel cartridges

Good knife with can opener; basic tool box

Maps and guides

Esky with ice packs

Fly net

Insect repellent

"Tyreseal"/tyre-fixing kit

Plastic box that can be used as both storage and table

Wrench, hammer, small axe

Hot water bottle / container

Metal kettle that can be put on fire or burner

Water-resistant clothing and shoes. As for the shoes: good sturdy trekking shoes might be too warm in the north but will become a life-saver in the south, especially when hiking in the mountains

Candles lighter, matches

Needle and thread/sewing kit
Large plastic bags
Air pump
Useful shops/sites:
>Car part supplies: Repco, AutoOne, Supercheapauto
>DIY/camping supplies: Bunnings, Mitre 10, Masters
>Electrical: Jaycar Electronics
>Mattresses: Clarke Rubber
>Large foodstore/grocery chains: Aldi (best value for money), Woolworths, Coles, Iga
>Non-grocery/camping: K-Mart, Target, Big W
>Miscellaneous/Discount: any "one dollar shop" in large shopping centres like Dollar King, Reject Shop etc.
>Second-hand items: Vinnies (St Vincent de Paul Society), Salvos (Salvation Army), Anglicare (Anglican Church)
>Cars: carsales.com.au, ozcar.com.au

Bibliography

Bailey, John. *White Divers of Broome (The true story of a fatal experiment)*. Sydney: Pan Macmillan Australia Pty Ltd, 2002.

Jas. S. Battye. The History of the North West of Australia. Perth, 1915

Haill, Robert G. *Opals of the Never Never.* Cammeray: Horwitz Grahame Books Pty Ltd, 1981.

Elwood, Paul. *Around Australia by Bicycle: The Complete Guide.* Elwood, Paul, 2003.

Drinkwater, M. *The German-Australian called Holtermann (Ein Deutsch-Australier namens Holtermann.* Sydney: Malcolm Drinkwater, 1985.

Baker, Robert G.V. *The Second Rush (A Study of the Second Goldrush to Sofala in 1851.* Cronulla: Centre Pak Research, 1986.

Thomas Tyrone T. *50 Walks in the Grampians.* Melbourne: Hill of Content, 1983.

Department of Environment and Conservation. *Karijini National Park Information and Walk Trail.*

Pilger, John. *A Secret Country*, London: Vintage, 1992.

Mundle, Rob. Flinders: The Man who Mapped Australia. Sydney: Hachette Australia Pty Limited, 2012.

Spencer, Sir Walter Baldwin. The Native Tribes of Central Australia: Adamant Media Corporation, 2000.

Phelps, James. Australia's Most Murderous Prison: Behind the Walls of Goulburn Jail. North Sydney: Random House Australia Pty. Ltd., 2015.

INDEX

A

Aboriginal paintings 120
Aboriginal rebels. *See* Jandamarra
Adelaide 174
Adelaide River 113
Adnyamathanha. *See* Wilpena Pound
Afghans 134
air con. *See* air conditioning
air conditioning 43
Alice Springs 129
Alice Springs Telegraph Station 130
Alpine National Park 196
ANZAC 109
ANZAC Day 108
Anzac Hill, Alice Springs 130
APC 128
April 25 108
Arrernte people 130
Atilla. *See* Mount Conner
ATMs 45
Australian "winter" 34
Ayers Rock. *See* Uluru

B

back-burning 115
Bana, Eric 191
Banjima Drive 61
Barramundi Gap 106
Barrow Creek 129
Bathurst 207
bats, Mataranka 124
Baudin, Commodore Nicholas 74
bends. *See* decompression disease
Bernard Holtermann. *See* Bernhardt Otto Holtermann
Bernhardt Otto Holtermann 212
Beyers, Hugo Luis 212
bicentenary 29

Big Aboriginal family, Wyndham 94
Big crocodile. Wyndham 93
Big Koala. *See* Giant Koala
Big Merino, Goulburn 203
Big Rocking Horse, Gumeracha 174
billabong 121
bindies 45
Binnu 50
Bird Rock, Grampians 181
bob trailer 71
Bowali Visitor Centre 118
Breakaways 150, 151
Bridle Track 207
Broome 71, 72, 73–80, 74
Broome, Sir Frederick Napier 78
Bufo Marinus. *See* cane toad
Buley Rock Hole 113
Bungle Bungle National Park 91
bush shower 67

C

cam belt 43
camel farm 134
Canberra 202
cane toad 72
Cape Range National Park 57
Carnarvon 55–54
Cathedral Termite Mound 113
cattle grid 49, 53
Centennial Park 190
Centipede 161
Charlie 199
China Wall 92
Chopper 187, 187–192
Clarke, William Branwhite 209
Colac Colac 195
common sense 62
Coober Pedy 151, 153–166
Cooinda 121
Cook, James 31
Coolangatta, QLD 107

Coral Bay 55
corn detasseling 97, 100
corrugated road 61
Costa d'Ouro 209
crocodile 95, 112, 118
crocodile farm, Kakadu 118
crocodile farm, Wyndham 94
Crossing Inn, pub 86
Cumberland River Holiday Park 186
Curtin Springs 140, 147
cyclone Tracy 115

D

Daly Waters 127
damper 166
Dampier, WA 66
Dampier, William 75
Dandenong Ranges 193
Darwin 83, 115
Darwin nude beach 115
Dead Horse Gap 196, 197
decompression disease 77
Devils Marbles 128, 129
diamond mine 106
dingo 69, 119
Dingo case 148–149
Diprotodon optatum 175
Dirt Holes Creek 210
Dodger. *See* Roger Dodger Rogerson
Douglas Hot Springs 112, 113
duty of care 63

E

Edith Falls 111
Elliot 127
El Questro 95
Elsey National Park 123
Elwood, Paul 71
Emma Gorge 95
emu 38, 57
Emu 167

Erldunda Caravan Park 135
Esplanade Hotel, Framantle 40
Exmouth Gulf 56

F

Falconio, Peter 129
false Uluru 140
Fitzroy Crossing 90
flies 129
Flinders, Matthew 171
Flinders Ranges. *See* Ikara-Flinders Ranges
Floriade 202
flying fox 123
Ford Falcon 35, 36, 84
Free Coffee for Driver 50, 128
Fremantle 39
Freo. *See* Fremantle
freshie, fresh water crocodile 103
fruit bat. *See* flying fox

G

Gallipoli 108
Gariwerd. *See* Grampians
Geiki Gorge 90
Geiki, Sir Archibald 90
Geraldton 49, 50
German Town 212
Ghan 126
Ghan Museum 134
giant kangaroo. *See* Procoptodon goliah
Giant Koala near Stawell 180
giant wombat. *See* Diprotodon optatum
Gibb River Road 95
Gillen, Francis James 130
Gipps, Sir George 209
Glow Worm Tunnel 206
Go, game 150
Gold 209
Golden Orb Spider 45
goon 74
Goulburn 202

Grampians 177–184
Grand Canyon, Grampians 179
Great Barrier Reef 56
Great Depression 155
Great Ocean Road 185
Gumeracha 174

H

half cast 76
Halls Creek 92
Halls Gap 178
Hamersley, Edward 64
Hamersley Ranges 64
Hancock Gorge 64
Hancock, Lang 59
Handrail Pool, Karijini 65
Hargraves, Edward Hammond 210
Havlik Park 113
Hayes Creek 112
Hidden Valley Caravan Park 115
Hill End 206, 207–216
History Hill 216
Holden 35, 37
Hollow Mountain, Grampians 179, 184
Holtermann, Otto Bernhardt 212
Huckstepp, Sallie-Anne 189
huntsman, spider 51
Hutchinson, Bill 155

I

Ikara. *See* Ikara-Flinders Ranges
Ikara-Flinders Ranges 169–173
indigenous 25, 29, 75, 158
inselberg 140
invasion 30
iron ore 64

J

Jabiru 118, 120
Jackie 199
Jandamarra 84

Japanese Cemetery in Broome 81
Jenolan Caves 204
Jindabyne 196
Joffre Falls 66
Joffre Gorge 64
Johns, Ronnie 192
junkyards 44, 119
Jurien Bay 48, 49

K

Kaiser Steel 60
Kakadu Highway 122
Kakadu National Park 116, 117–121
kamikaze 81
Kanangra Boyd 204
kangaroos 44, 57, 59–239
karaoke 110
Karijini 60
Karijini Drive 64, 69
Karijini gorges
  Hancock Gorge 64
  Joffre Gorge 64
  Knox Gorge 65
  Red Gorge 65
  Weano Gorge 64
  Wittenoom Gorge 65
Karijini National Park 64
Karlstein castle 113
Karlu Karlu. *See* Devils Marbles
Kata Tjuta 139, 141, 146
Katherine Gorge 110
Kelly, Ned 188
Kimberley Range 77
Kings Canyon 139, 146, 147
Kings Canyon Rim Walk 147
Knox Gorge 65
kookaburra 39
Kulgera 150
Kununurra 96–100

L

Lake Argyle 101–105, 107
Lake Eyre 170
Lake Hart 170
Lanfranchi, Warren 189
Larapinta Trail 130, 133
Lasseter Highway 142
Lees, Joanne 129
Lenin's tomb 125
Leopold Downs Road 84
Lister, John 210
Litchfield National Park 113–114
London Bridge 185

M

Mabo case 34
Mabo, Eddie Koiki 30, 32
Mad Max 150
Malabanjbandju Caravan Area 118, 120
Mala Walk Parking Area 144
Mango Camping Area 78
Maralinga 167
Mary Ann Dam 128
Mataranka 122
Mataranka airstrip 125
Matsu Range 106
Mawson Peak 196
McArthur, James 199
McBrien, James 209
Melbourne 187
Melbourne Cup 80
Mendeleev, Dmitri 209
Milat, Ivan 88–89
Mindil Beach Sunset Market 115
missionaries 33
Monaghan's Bluff 207
monsoon rain 53
Moscow 125
mosquitoes 118, 120
mother-of-pearl 74
Mount Bruce 66, 67, 69
Mount Buffalo 195

Mount Conner 140
Mount Ebenezer Roadhouse 140, 147
Mount Kosciuszko 196–200
Mount McClintock 196
Mount Meharry 69
Mount Menzies 196
Mount Nameless 69
Mount Sonder 132, 133
Mount Stapylton 180, 181
Mount Townsend 198
Mudgee 207
Murdoch, Bradley John 129
Murray Island, Queensland 32

N

Nambung National Park 48
nanny state 62
Naracoorte 175
NASA 102, 144
Native Title to Land 33
nerve test 178
New Holland 31, 199
Newnes 205
New South Wales 195
Ngariro Campground 197
Ngarri Mudlanha. *See* St Mary Peak
Ningaloo Marine Park 56
Nitmiluk National Park 110
noodling 130
noodling machinery 164
North West Cape Peninsula 56
Nourlangie Rock Art Site 120

O

Ochre Pits 131
octopus as God 33
OH&S 104
Oil shell refinery 205
oil-shell rock 205
Old Ghan 135
Olgas. *See* Kata Tjuta

Onions, Paul 88–89
opal 130, 154
Ophir 210
Orange 210
Ormiston Campground 131
Ormiston Gorge 131
ostrich 38

P

Paraburdoo 58, 64
Pavlova, ballerina 41
Pavlova, cake 42
permanent residency 86
Perth 39
Petersham 190
petrol stations 43
Phillip, Arthur 29
Pierce, Alexander 188
Pinnacles 48, 50
Port Augusta 169, 170
Port Hedland 69, 71, 72
possum 39
potch 156, 157, 163, 164
Potter's Sanctuary 194
Pound Walk 131, 132
Price, Thomas Moore 60
Procoptodon goliah 176
Pteropus. *See* flying fox
Purnululu. *See* Bungle Bungle National Park

R

Read, Mark Brandon Chopper 188
redback. spider 38
Redbank Gorge 132
Red Centre 134, 139–147
Red Gorge 65
Reservoir Dogs 191
rest places 44
Ricketts, William 193
Riley, James 199
Rio Tinto 106

Rocket park, Woomera 167
"Rocky Open Legs" 146
Roger Dodger Rogerson 189
"R-rated Ladies' Privates Rock" 146
Rwetyepme. *See* Mount Sonder

S

saltie, salt water crocodile 103
Sandfire Roadhouse 72
Sandy Billabong, tragedy 121
Savannah campground, Karijini 66
Sex on the Beach 161
Sexy Walls 146
Shady Glen Caravan Park 115
sheep 49, 177, 185, 203
sheep dog 177
Shipwreck Coast 186
Shithouse, Daly Waters 127
Shore, Anglican private school 214
shovel-nosed catfish. *See* silver cobbler
Silent Street, Grampians 179
silver cobbler, fish 106
Simpsons Gap 130
Snowy Mountains 195
Sow and Piglets 186
spear-thrower, Woomera 167
Spencer, Sir Walter Baldwin 130
spiders
  Golden Orb Spider 45
  huntsman 51
  redback 38
spinifex 78
Squashed Frog 161
"squirrelcats" 39
Star of Hope 213
Stawell 178
St Mary Peak 173
stolen generation 76
Strzelecki, Sir Edmund 209
Strzelecki, Sir Paul Edmund 199
Stuart Highway 112, 122

Stuart, John McDuall 112
Stuart Range 151
Sydney, First Viscount 198
Sydney Harbour Bridge 215

T

Tambaroora 210
Tarunda Caravan Park 85
Telstra 45
Tennant Creek 128
terra nullius 31
thongs 45
Thredbo 197
Three Ways 128
timing belt. *See* cam belt
Tjuwaliyn. *See* Douglas Hot Springs
Todd River 130
Tom, James 210
Tom Price 58, 59
Townsend, Thomas 198
Toyota Corolla 36
trekking bike 136
tucker 75
Tunnel Creek 84
Turkey Creek 91
Turon River 210

U

Uluru 129, 137, 139, 141, 146

V

Valley of the Winds 146
Vlaming Head 57

W

Wakayama province 79
Walpa Gorge Walk 146
Warmun Roadhouse 91
Weano Gorge 64
West MacDonnell Ranges 130–134

White Australia policy 79
Wilpena Pound 172
Windjana Gorge 84
Wintersun Caravan Park 129
Wittenoom Gorge 65
Wolfe Creek Crater 92
Wollemia nobilis. *See* Wollemi Pine
Wollemi National Park 204
Wollemi Pine 204
Woomera 166
work and holiday visa 54
Work and Holiday visa 86
Wyndham 93

Y

YAK-52, aircraft 125
Yardie Creek 57, 58
Yorkies Creek 210
Yulara 142, 146, 147

Z

zebra rock 106

www.ingramcontent.com/pod-product-compliance
Lightning Source LLC
Chambersburg PA
CBHW030438300426
44112CB00009B/1064